I0810188

INDIGENOUS REPATRIATION HANDBOOK

Prepared by
Jisgang Nika Collison,
Sdaahl K'awaas Lucy Bell
and Lou-ann Neel

ROYAL BC MUSEUM

HAIDA GWAII MUSEUM AT KAY LLNAGAAY

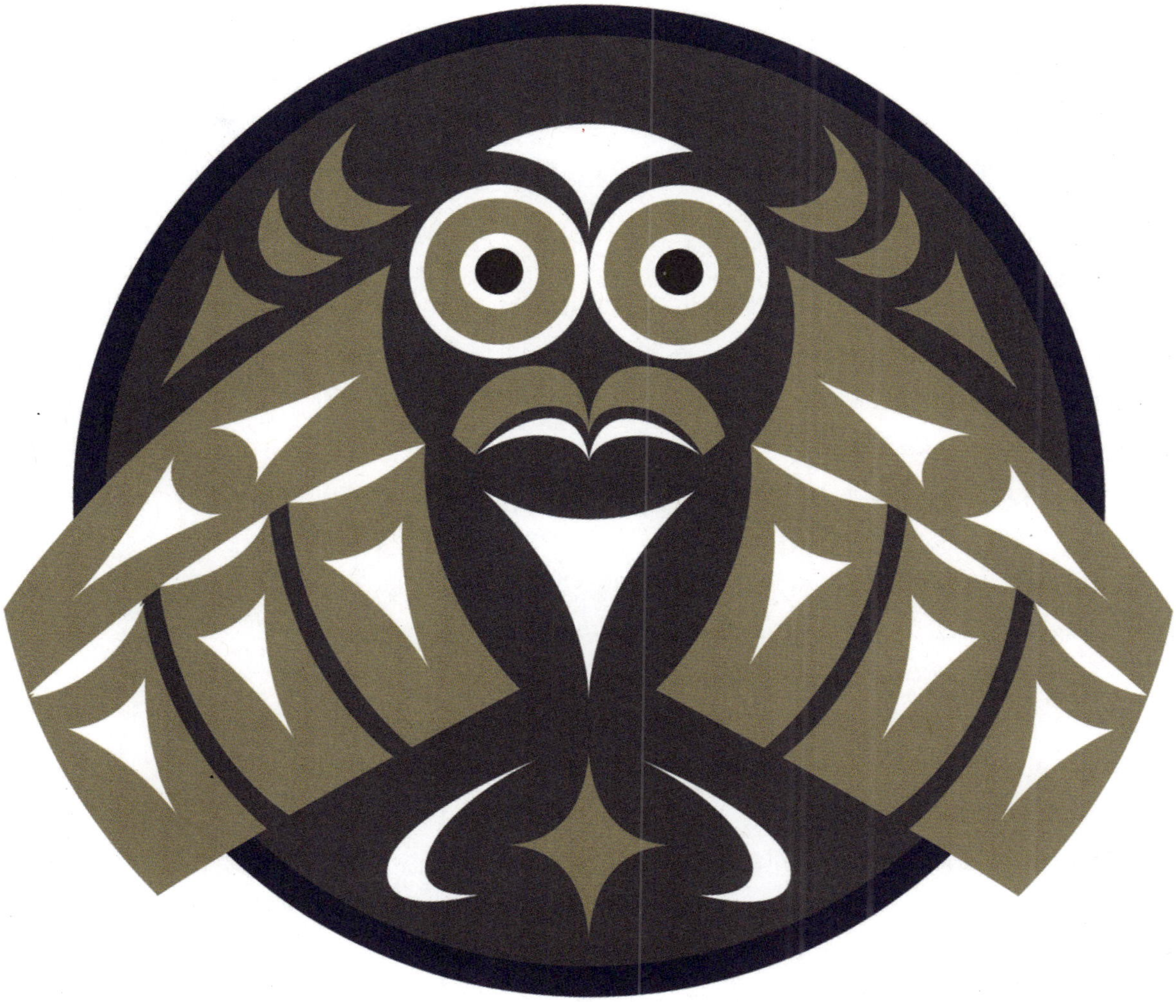

Indigenous Repatriation Handbook

Prepared by Jisgang Nika Collison, Sdaahl K̲'awaas Lucy Bell and Lou-ann Neel

Published by the Royal BC Museum, 675 Belleville Street,
Victoria, British Columbia, V8W 9W2, Canada.
Traditional territory of the Lekwungen (Songhees and Xwsepsum Nations).

Interior design and typesetting by Nathan Oickle and Jeff Werner
Cover artwork by Dylan Thomas
Cover design by Fresh Art & Design Inc.
Interior artwork by Margaret Briere
All photographs courtesy of the Royal BC Museum unless otherwise noted

Library and Archives Canada Cataloguing in Publication
Title: Indigenous repatriation handbook / prepared by Jisgang Nika Collison, Sdaahl K'awaas Lucy Bell and Lou-ann Neel.
Names: Collison, Jisgang Nika, 1971- author. | Bell, Sdaahl K'awaas Lucy, 1971- author. | Neel, Lou-ann, 1963- author. | Royal British Columbia Museum, publisher.
Description: Includes bibliographical references.
Identifiers: Canadiana (print) 20190084634 | Canadiana (ebook) 20190085126 | ISBN 9780772673176 (softcover) | ISBN 9780772673183 (PDF)
Subjects: LCSH: Indians of North America—Material culture—British Columbia—Handbooks, manuals, etc. | LCSH: Cultural property—Repatriation—British Columbia—Handbooks, manuals, etc.
Classification: LCC E98.M34 C65 2019 | DDC 971.1004/97—dc23

TABLE OF CONTENTS

ACKNOWLEDGEMENTS

The authors thank everyone who made this handbook possible, including:

- Province of British Columbia Ministry of Tourism, Arts & Culture
- Tracey Herbert and the First Peoples' Cultural Council
- Vince Collison of the Haida Gwaii Museum at K̲ay Llnagaay
- The Haida Repatriation Committee
- Dr. Genevieve Hill, Katie Dierks, Brooke Albers, Genevieve Weber, Emma Wright and Erika Stenson of the Royal British Columbia Museum
- Dr. Laura Peers
- Honor Keeler
- The speakers from the 2017 Indigenous Perspectives on Repatriation Symposium
- The museums, archives, cultural centres and associations mentioned in the handbook
- The 2018 Royal BC Museum Repatriation Grant recipients

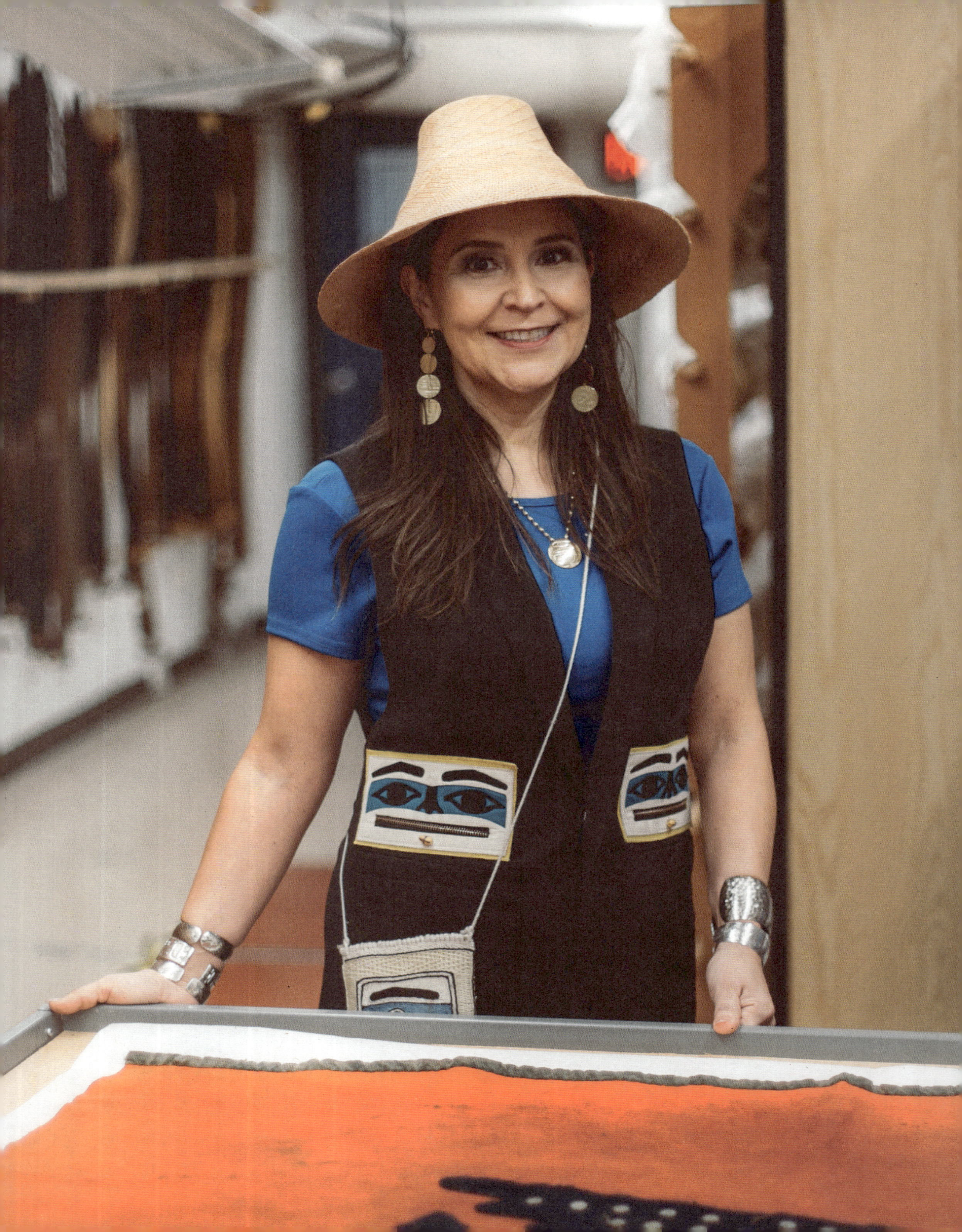

MESSAGE FROM

Lucy Bell, Head of the Indigenous Collections and Repatriation Department, Royal BC Museum

Lucy Bell, head of the Indigenous Collections and Repatriation Department, in the Indigenous Collections and Repatriation area. Photo courtesy University of Victoria Alumni Relations.

Singaay 'laas, dii tuwiilang, it gives me great pleasure to share with you the *Indigenous Repatriation Handbook*! This handbook sure would have been handy at the beginning of my repatriation journey, but it gives me great pride and hope for you as you begin your own.

I raise my hands to everyone who made the handbook a reality. The Royal BC Museum staff, the Haida Gwaii Museum at K̲ay Llnagaay, the First Peoples' Cultural Council and the 2018 Royal BC Museum Repatriation Grant recipients did a wonderful job of bringing this valuable resource together.

I also give thanks to my handbook collaborators, Jisgang Nika Collison and Lou-ann Neel. The three of us worked diligently to ensure this was a thorough resource. We have extensive experience in museology, administration, research and repatriation. We have also walked between our Indigenous worlds and mainstream museum worlds, and we know how challenging and rewarding this work can be. We hope our reflections and suggestions are helpful to you.

Dii k'anguudanggang. I am hopeful! We are in a new era of reconciliation that involves repatriation and creating meaningful relationships between museums and Indigenous communities. I am proud of the strides we have all made, and I look forward to witnessing the new possibilities!

I wish you well on your repatriation journey, and I look forward to learning about your repatriation successes.

Dalang aa Hl kil 'laagang,
Lucy Bell
Sdaahl K̲'awaas

MESSAGE FROM

Professor Jack Lohman CBE, Chief Executive Officer, Royal BC Museum, and Tracey Herbert, CEO, First Peoples' Cultural Council

On behalf of the Royal BC Museum and the First Peoples' Cultural Council, it is our pleasure to share this new resource with Indigenous communities and museum professionals around the province.

The *Indigenous Repatriation Handbook* is made possible by the generous support of the Province of British Columbia and through a partnership with the Haida Gwaii Museum at K̲ay Llnagaay, with guidance from the First Peoples' Cultural Council and the Royal BC Museum Indigenous Advisory and Advocacy Committee.

Informed by Indigenous people, the 1992 Task Force on Museums and First Peoples, the 1996 Royal Commission on Aboriginal Peoples, the 2007 United Nations Declaration on the Rights of Indigenous Peoples, and the 2015 Truth and Reconciliation Commission's 94 Calls to Action, the handbook also helps to outline the important steps the Royal BC Museum is taking to honour these policy frameworks through the new Indigenous Collections and Repatriation Policy and the museum's 2019–2022 strategic plan.

With 34 unique Indigenous language and cultural groups in BC, this handbook seeks to provide practical information that will enable each group to carry out the process of repatriation in ways that align with the cultural traditions of each respective community, while also providing information that will be helpful to museums.

Tsilhqot'in basket, RBCM 2800.

We recognize that the handbook will undergo ongoing transformation as new information, processes, policies and practices unfold, and we hope you will find this first edition a useful starting point. We welcome and invite your feedback through the Indigenous Collections and Repatriation Department at the Royal BC Museum.

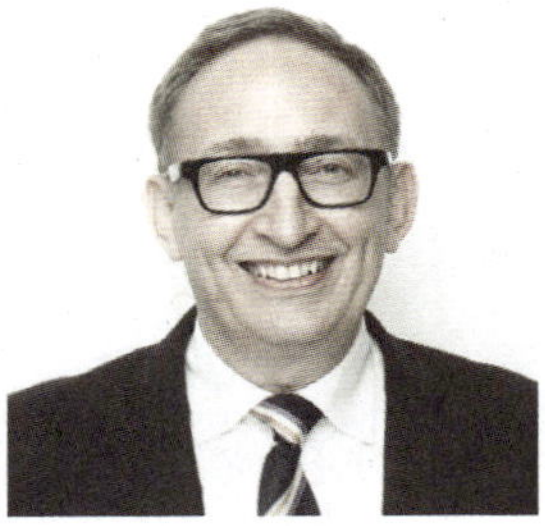

Professor Jack Lohman CBE, CEO,
Royal BC Museum

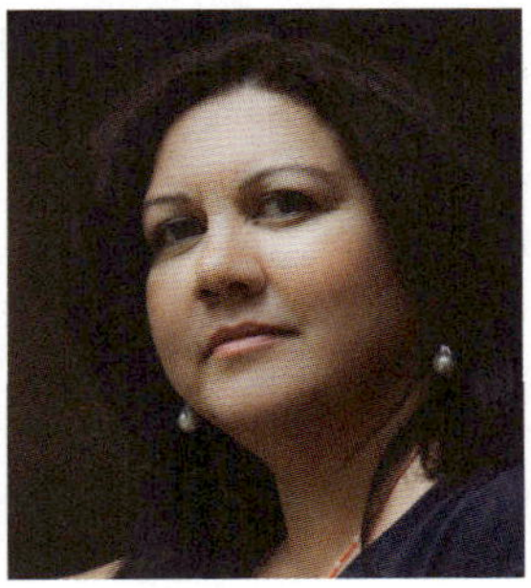

Tracey Herbert, CEO,
First Peoples' Cultural Council

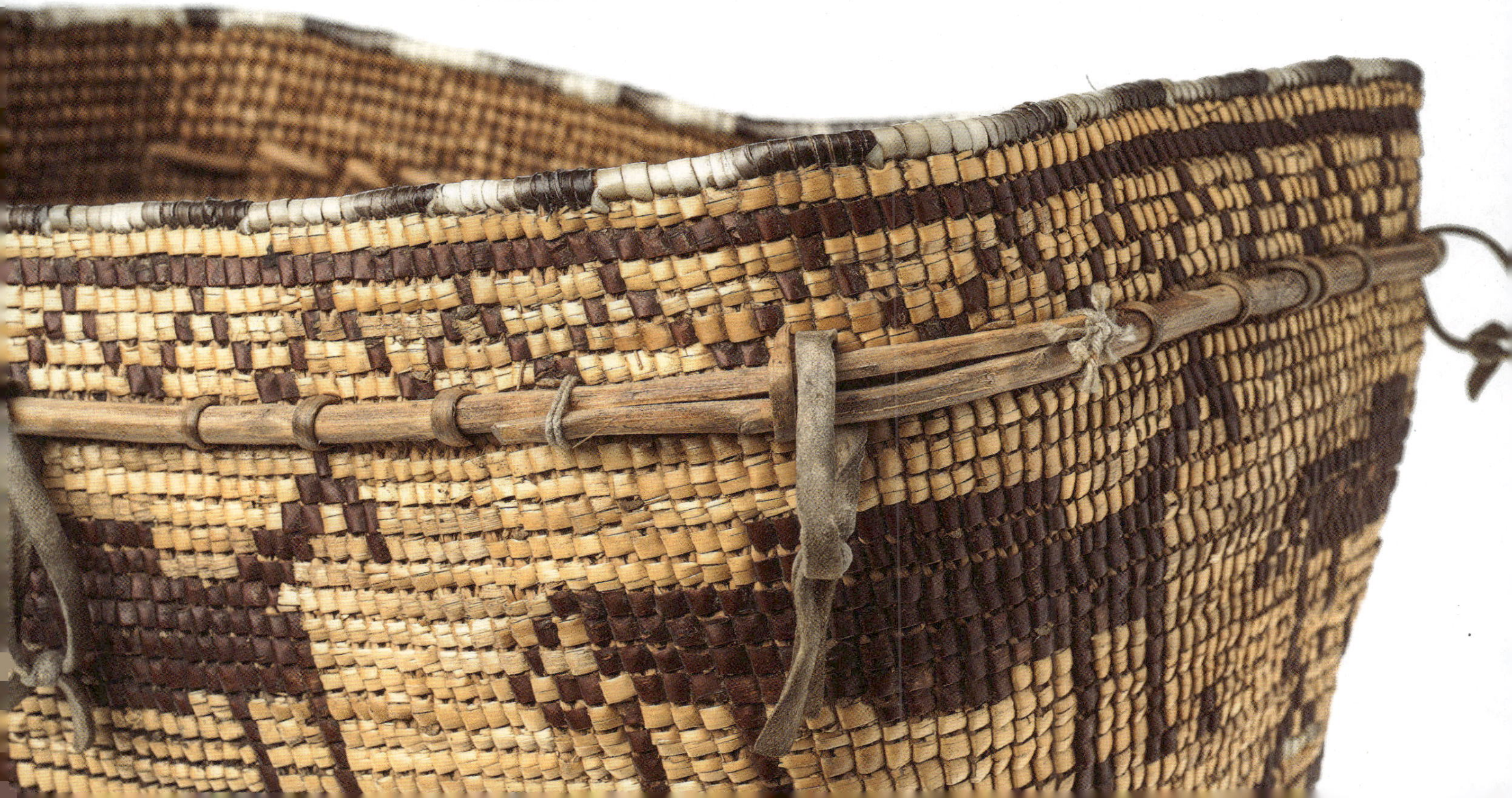

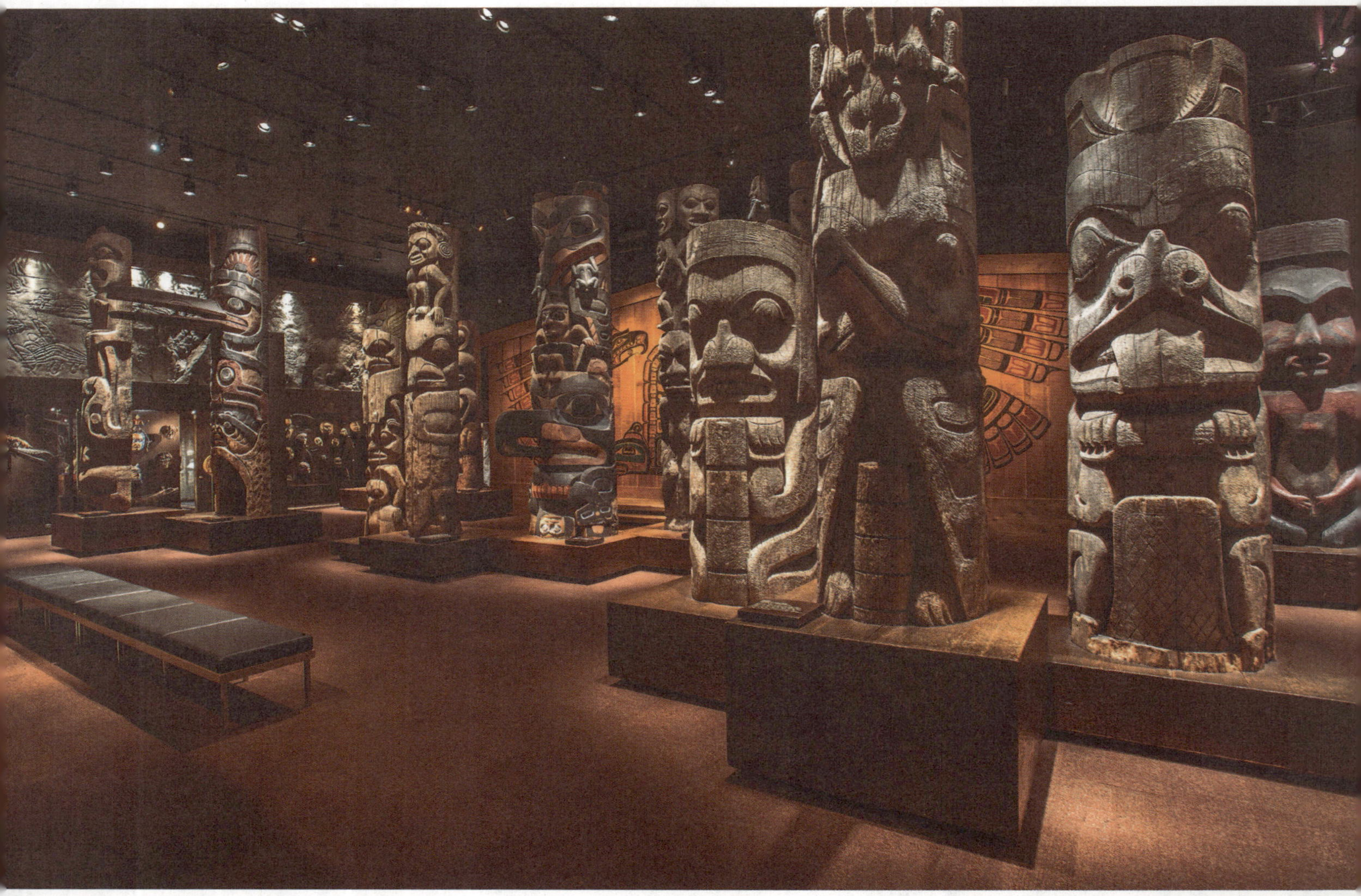

The Totem Hall at the RBCM.

PART 1

Introduction

Welcome to the *Indigenous Repatriation Handbook*.

This first edition of the handbook was written by the Indigenous Collections and Repatriation Department of the Royal BC Museum and the Haida Gwaii Museum at Kay Llnagaay, and it was reviewed by the First Peoples' Cultural Council and the Royal BC Museum Indigenous Advisory and Advocacy Committee.

The handbook was created in response to the feedback received during the 2017 Repatriation Symposium hosted by the Royal BC Museum and the First Peoples' Cultural Council. The forum brought together over 200 delegates from Indigenous communities throughout British Columbia, as well as representatives of museums and government agencies from around the world. Participants of the forum recommended the creation of a handbook that would support communities and museums that are in the beginning stages of planning for repatriation in BC and at national and international levels.

Repatriation is not just a word, but a call to action.

~ Jordan Coble, Sncewips Heritage Museum

To repatriate something is to return it to the country of its origin. For museums, repatriation applies more specifically to the return of human remains and cultural objects to Indigenous communities. Because the process of repatriation is different in each instance, we envision that this handbook will continue to evolve and transform as newer practices, policies and processes are developed.

The content of this first edition is based on the knowledge and experiences of a number of Indigenous communities in BC, as well as staff of the Royal BC Museum, who collectively have been working on repatriation for the past 30 or more years. The handbook is meant to serve as a reference and is not intended to be prescriptive; rather, it provides guidance on activities related to the process of repatriation.

Our late friend and brother Rod Naknakim said, "Reconciliation and repatriation cannot and should not be separated. The two must anchor our conversation and guide our efforts as we move forward collectively with common purpose and understanding."

~ Dan Smith, BC Museums Association Indigenous Advisory Chair, Nuyumbalees Cultural Centre

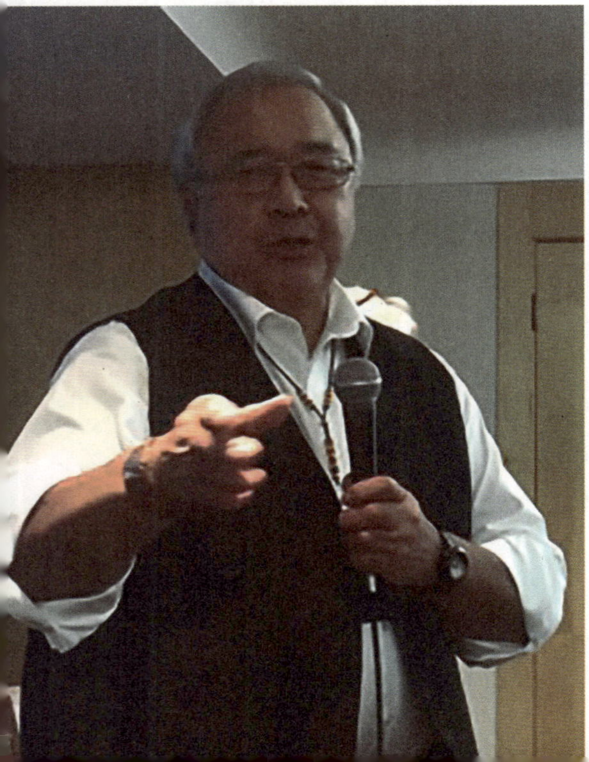

Dan Smith speaks about the Rod Naknakim repatriation declaration at the BC Museums Association conference.

If your community or museum is interested in sharing case studies, samples, templates or any other ideas for the handbook, please contact Lou-ann Neel, repatriation specialist at the Royal BC Museum, by emailing lneel@royalbcmuseum.bc.ca.

The *Indigenous Repatriation Handbook* is available online at RBCM.ca/RepatriationBook.

How to Use This Handbook

The *Indigenous Repatriation Handbook* was created to serve as a handy reference for Indigenous Nations in BC and mainstream museums involved in the process of repatriation. It is important to note that it was created by and for Indigenous people working in repatriation.

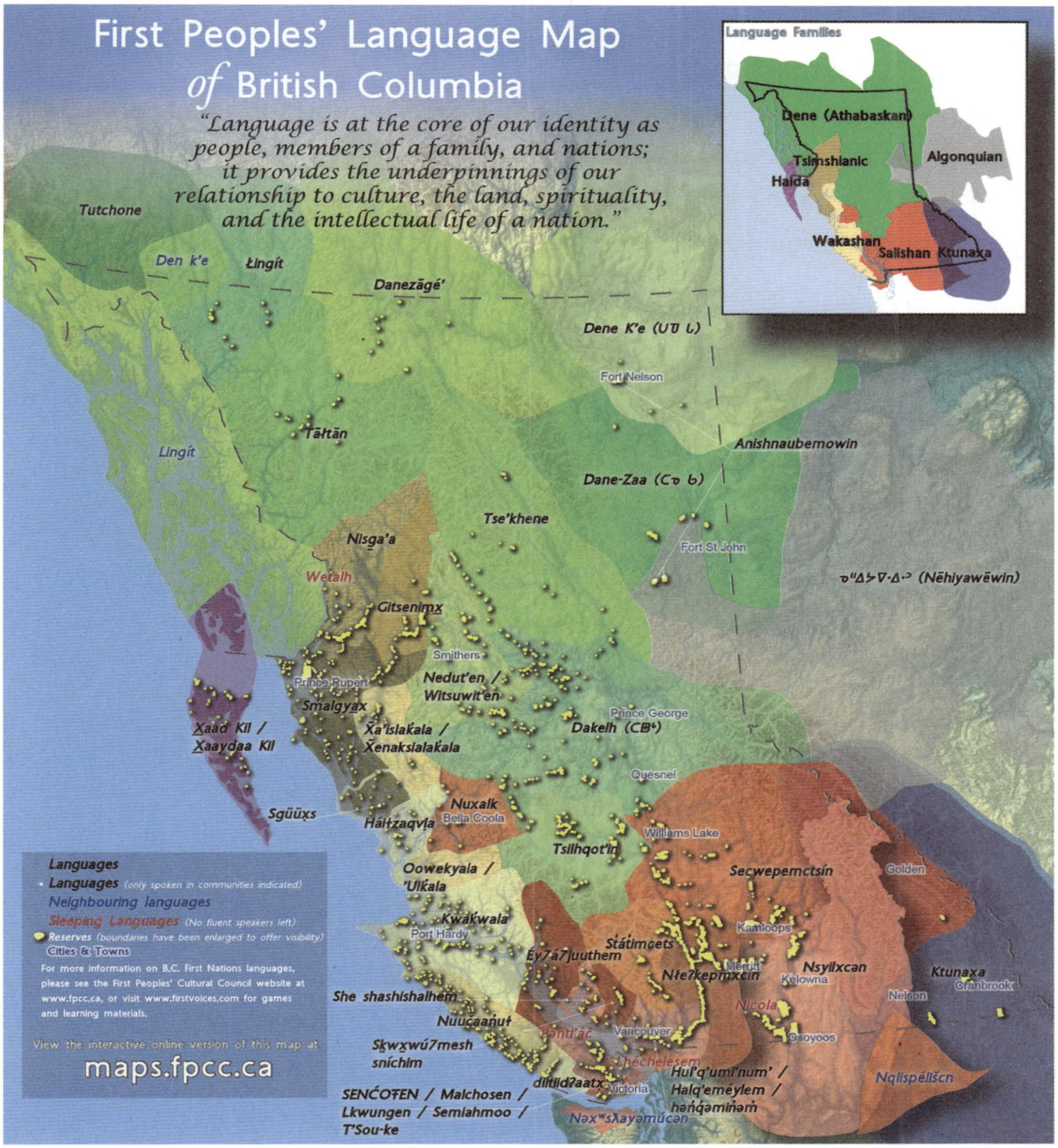

Map of Indigenous language groups in British Columbia. Map courtesy of the First Peoples' Cultural Council.

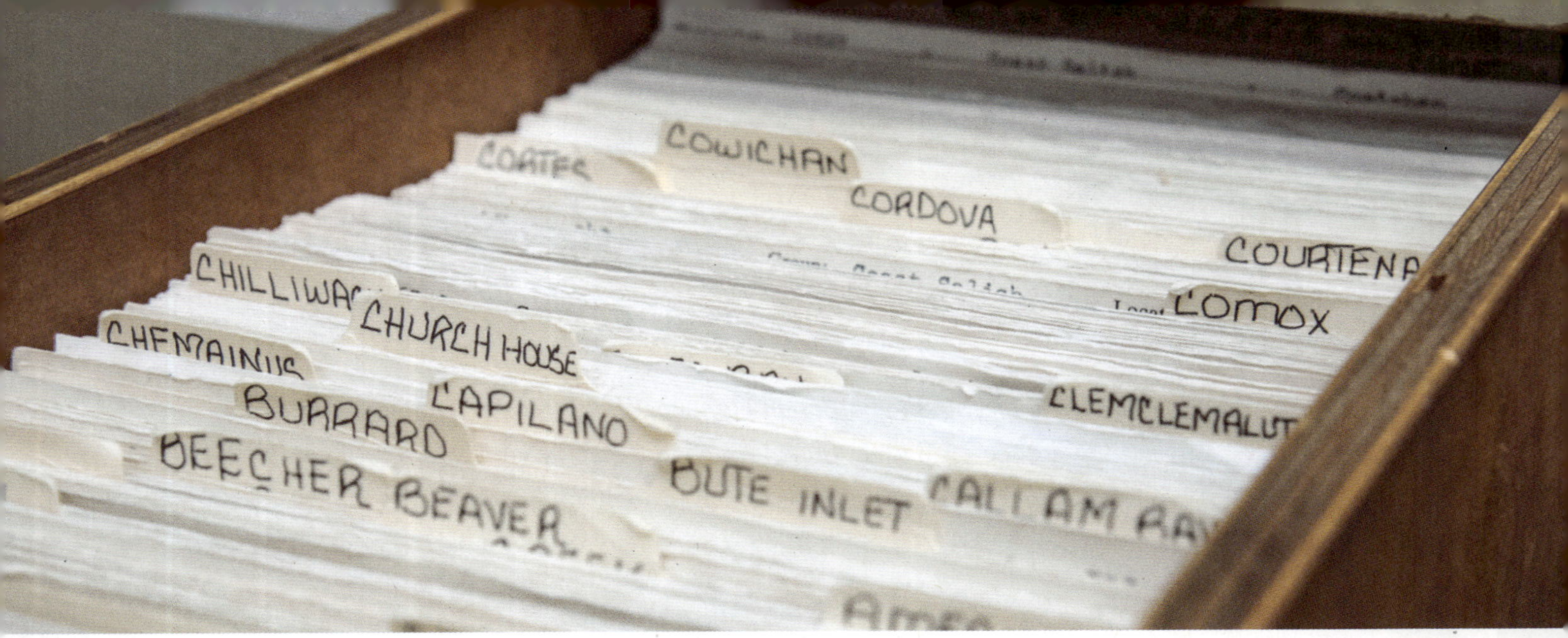

Audiovisual collection photo index cards, organized in drawers by cultural linguistic group and location.

The handbook is divided into seven parts, each with a topic heading, brief overview, background or historical information about the topic, and the most current information and online links available. Each section stands alone, so you can just read the information that applies to you. Part 1: Introduction sets the historical context of repatriation. Part 2: Organizing a Successful Repatriation and Part 3: Conducting Research provide practical guidance for Nations planning and researching repatriation. Part 4: Repatriation from the Royal BC Museum and Part 5: Repatriation from other Institutions give specific information on repatriating from the Royal BC Museum and other museums around the world. Part 6: For Institutions Wishing to Repatriate to Indigenous Peoples in BC looks at how museums themselves can initiate and carry out repatriation. Finally, Part 7: Case Study: Repatriation Journey of the Haida Nation is a case study that presents the repatriation experience of the Haida Nation, illustrating a real-life example of the guidance given in this handbook.

In the appendices are samples and templates that can be downloaded for use by communities and museums. All can be customized to suit the unique needs of each community. There is also a glossary of common repatriation-related terms (Appendix A: Glossary of Terms), additional information on global institutions (Appendix G: Global Museums with Major Indigenous Collections from BC), and lists of further resources (Appendix D: Fundraising Resources and Appendix H: Resources on Education in Indigenous Museology).

Historical Context and Museums and Archives Today

This section provides a brief history of how Indigenous Ancestors and belongings in BC wound up in museums, universities and private collections. We recognize that the shared history of Indigenous Nations, BC and Canada is far more complex and multi-layered than can be fully explored here, and that each Nation has their own history to tell. Check the glossary in Appendix A: Glossary of Terms if you come across words you don't recognize.

A Bit about Museums and Archives

The traditional role of museums is to collect objects and materials of cultural, religious and historical importance, preserve them, research them and present them to the public for the purpose of education and enjoyment. The first known museum was created during the third century CE at the University of Alexandria in Egypt.[1] Today there are over 55,000 museums in the world.[2]

Museums come in many sizes and forms, such as community and regional museums, university museums, public art museums and galleries, and national or state museums (i.e., government-run institutions with a mandate to collect, preserve and present nation-state histories). Some museums might be the size of a classroom; others take up a city block or have more than one building around town; still others are virtual. Some are focused on very specific topics, while others have broader mandates.

1 Emmanuel N. Arinze, President, Commonwealth Association of Museums, public lecture at the National Museum, Georgetown, Guyana, May 17, 1999. Available at maltwood.uvic.ca/cam/activities/past_conferences/1999conf/CAM%2799-EmmanuelArinze.GuyanaFinal.pdf

2 *Museums of the World* (Berlin: De Gruyter, 2011).

National museums and other institutions with a natural or human history mandate, as well as some universities, are the institutions that most often hold Indigenous belongings from around the world, from basic day-to-day utensils to the highest of ceremonial items and everything in between. Many of these institutions also hold Indigenous Ancestral remains.

Archives, which are where valuable records and objects are kept, often contain great amounts of intangible Indigenous heritage, preserved in the forms of oral history and song recordings, video footage, photographs, drawings, written records and so on. Universities and most museums usually have some form of library and archive. Sometimes archives are run as standalone institutions.

Canada's national museum is the Canadian Museum of History in Gatineau, Quebec, while its national archive, Library and Archives Canada, is in Ottawa, Ontario. The Royal BC Museum is BC's provincial museum, which was joined by the BC Provincial Archives in 2003.

How Did Indigenous Ancestors and Belongings Wind Up in Museums?

Museums are amazing places of wonder and education. They provide opportunity for the general public to see and learn about people, places, things and ideas that might not have been accessible otherwise. But Indigenous people don't always feel this way about mainstream museum experiences. This is because a great many of the Indigenous treasures in museum collections were acquired during a very dark time in the history of Indigenous Peoples and the nation-state of Canada.

North America had been home to Indigenous people for millennia by the time the British and other Europeans began to arrive on the east coast of what is today called Canada. On the west coast, interactions between Indigenous people and settlers began in the latter half of the 1700s. Early relationships were mainly economy based (though not without conflict), and in BC, were largely driven by the maritime fur trade (ca. 1790–1840). Indigenous people traded their furs, food,

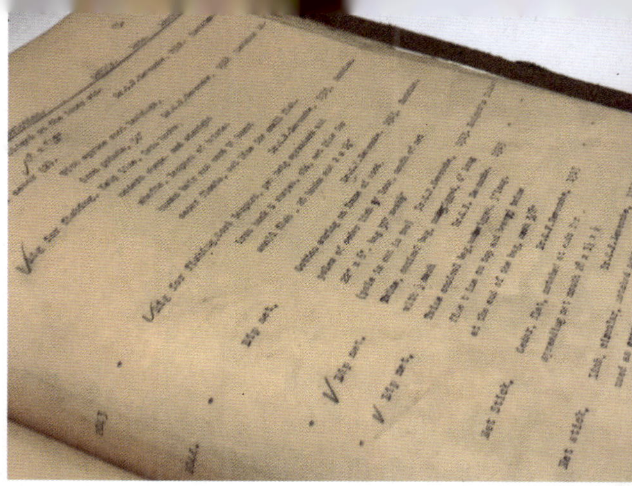

RBCM catalogue of cultural treasures.

commercial art and even some personal belongings, among other things, in exchange for iron, wool blankets and other exotic materials, including some personal belongings of the foreign traders. As the fur trade waned, British colonizers began seeking new resource-based economies and the land itself. Relations between the two worlds had already become complicated at this point, but things were about to get much worse.

Along with foreign people came foreign epidemics, which drastically impacted Indigenous Peoples, decimating their populations by as much as 90 per cent or more—wiping out entire families, villages and sometimes even Nations. Following the devastating impacts of several smallpox epidemics, missionaries were able to entrench themselves within surviving Indigenous communities with the goal of converting them to Christianity.

In 1876, the Canadian government passed the Indian Act, with the intent of assimilating Indigenous people into Canadian society and erasing Indigenous identity, rights and territories. This included making Indigenous people wards of the state, removing them from their expansive territories and putting them on tiny reserves, and creating "legal" mechanisms for Indigenous disenfranchisement. In 1884, the Indian Act was amended to render the Potlatch and other traditional cultural ceremonies illegal, which ultimately outlawed the social, economic and legal systems of Indigenous Peoples in BC, with "offenders" facing confiscation of their treasures as well as imprisonment. The Potlatch Ban was quietly dropped during a revision to the Act in 1951.

In 1892, Canada's residential school system was formalized, removing children from their homes. It denied Indigenous children their lands, language, family and greater community for most of their childhood, and subjected many to abuse or even death (thousands of children died in residential schools). The last residential school in Canada only closed in 1996.

Hand in hand with colonial regimes came a collecting frenzy and the birth of (then-modern) anthropology. Nation-state museums and world fairs were hungry for collections representing Indigenous people and their cultures. By the 1880s, colonizers were actively "collecting" Indigenous people and heritage as they pleased, asserting that Indigenous Nations and cultures were going extinct, and that our existence and way of life should be "collected" in the "interest of science" and preserved for the "benefit of humanity."

There was also notoriety and revenue to be gained in the field of collecting. Land surveyors, anthropologists and others were commissioned by nation-state governments and institutions to collect Indigenous heritage. There were also independents who dealt in "Indian curios," buying and selling to museums, collectors and other dealers. Museums also "dealt" in the open art market: buying and selling Indigenous heritage with great freedom. The Ancestors and belongings that were taken from Indigenous communities were traded around the world, most landing in museum and university collections, some others in private collections.

The height of what was ultimately unethical and often illegal collecting occurred between the latter half of the 1800s and the first half of the 1900s, though the practice carried on in a quieter manner through the 1970s and '80s. Indigenous graves were desecrated, with human remains and burial goods stolen. Personal belongings were taken by theft, force or "sale." Purchase records from this period document what one could perceive as "legitimate" sales of personal belongings by Indigenous people. However, given the circumstances of these times, it should be understood and accepted that most of these transactions occurred under duress, particularly sales that occurred during the Potlatch Ban era.

Unethical collecting still occurs today. Some cultural belongings and Ancestral remains are still being stolen or bought under duress and sold on the black market. It is important to become aware of the collecting that is still happening and to educate community members about this, so that the old belongings in the community do not disappear.

More recently, archaeological belongings and Ancestral remains have also ended up in museums as a result of archaeological excavations and recovery by the RCMP. Archaeology as a discipline began to take off in the 1960s, and since that time, all archaeological material recovered under permit is required to be sent to repositories (many of which were also museums). This material includes archaeological belongings and Ancestral materials as well as maps, photos, field notes, animal bones and soil samples. In these cases, the documentation is often very good.

In some cases, Ancestral material was sent to the Royal BC Museum and other museums by the RCMP. If human remains were reported to the RCMP, and were not of current forensic interest, they were turned over to the provincial museum. In cases such as these, the documentation can range from very general to quite specific.

I too am haunted not just by these displaced remains, but by every treasure that has left Indigenous Nations in today's British Columbia. Where are all these missing collections? Who has these artifacts? Are they just sitting somewhere? Well, they're not quite missing, these objects. They're just in the wrong place.

~ Jack Lohman CBE, CEO, Royal BC Museum

Changes in Mainstream Museums

Many museum people in North America, and a growing number overseas, are pretty easy to get along with in this day and age, but 20 years ago it was hard to get through the doors of some museums in Canada, let alone in the United States or farther abroad. For those working on relationship-building and repatriation overseas, it's really only been about 10 years since more than a handful of museums began opening their doors to Indigenous Peoples.

> ***As museum professionals, and as human beings, we carry the responsibility to affect societal change by mainstreaming Canada's dark history with Indigenous people while actively working to set things right. In the Haida Museum realm, the path toward conciliation has been shaped by Yahguudangang—the act of paying respect. The Haida Nation sees this work, which includes repatriation, as based upon mutual respect, cooperation and trust.***[3]
>
> ~ Jisgang Nika Collison, Executive Director,
> Haida Gwaii Museum at K̲ay Llnagaay

While there is a long way to go in working with museums to Indigenize their institutions, there have been significant changes over

3 Jennifer Shannon, Sonya Atalay, Jisgang Nika Collison, Te Herekiekie Herewini, Eric Hollinger, Michelle Horwood, Robert W. Preucel, Anthony Shelton and Paul Tapsell, "Ritual Processes of Repatriation: A Discussion," *Museum Worlds* 5 (1): 89–90, https://doi.org/10.3167/armw.2017.050109

years. We credit this to the Indigenous artists, Elders, researchers, collaborators, diplomats and repatriators across the lands who have tirelessly knocked on doors until they opened. But it takes both sides, so here is a shout out to the museum champions who were ready to listen and find ways to make changes in their institutions.

The Rise of Indigenous Museology

In the 1960s, some Indigenous communities in BC began looking at how to preserve and strengthen their cultural heritage through repatriation and Indigenous museology. In the process, new collectors and museums began to emerge: Indigenous ones!

The 'Ksan Historical Village and Museum (ksan.org) opened its doors in 1970 out of a desire to "preserve and truthfully portray the lifestyle of the people who have always lived here." The Haida Gwaii Museum (haidagwaiimuseum.ca) opened in 1976 with Haida Gwaii as its mandate. Today it is a partner of the Haida Heritage Centre at K̲ay Llnagaay (haidaheritagecentre.net), which opened in 2007. The Kwakwa̲ka̲'wakw opened two centres: the Nuyumbalees Cultural Centre (nuyumbalees.com, 1979) and the U'mista Cultural Centre (umista.ca, 1980) to house the Potlatch Collection their people repatriated.

Today there are several Indigenous-run museums as well as cultural education centres in BC that work with their communities and Nations to celebrate, protect and foster their respective languages, arts, cultures and heritage, and to house their repatriated belongings among other heirlooms, as well as newly created works (see Appendix B: Indigenous Museums and Cultural Centres in Canada). The beauty of an Indigenous museum is that communities can adapt mainstream museum practices to what works best for cultural practices and protocols.

Creating a museum or cultural centre is not the answer for every Indigenous Nation, however, and should not be required in order to bring home your belongings. Some communities might choose to enter into shared-ownership agreements with the museums that hold their collections; others might strike partnerships with local museums to house their repatriated belongings. Some communities choose to display their belongings in their band office or school. Others may forge entirely new paths that may or may not involve a formal institution. Still others may have members who wind up working in a mainstream museum, Indigenizing the institution from within.

It's honouring the artifacts as if they are living people. They have spirit to them. When people come into our museum, what we emphasize is that everything around us—and picture yourself in our museum right now—is alive.

~ Jordan Coble, Sncewips Heritage Museum

PART 2

Organizing a Successful Repatriation

If you are interested in repatriation, a great place to start is this handbook. Congratulations, you are already on your way! Bringing home your Ancestors and cultural heritage can be a big undertaking, but for many Indigenous Nations, this work has contributed greatly to their healing from the past; the preservation and continuation of their language, art and culture; and finding and forging paths toward reconciliation, among other things.

It may seem like an overwhelming and sometimes confusing task to figure out how to get started on the path to repatriation, but thankfully, there are a number of Indigenous communities who have shared some of the things that have worked for them. This section presents some of the steps and practices these communities have shared, and it is supplemented by the samples, templates and tips in Appendix C: Organizational Templates, Procedures and Examples, Appendix D: Fundraising Resources, Appendix E: Sample Letters to Museums and Appendix F: Tips for Planning for Travel and Transport.

Getting your house in order is the first key to success. How an Indigenous Nation gathers, organizes and implements the work of repatriation will depend on its own needs and ways of being in the world, but this section provides some tips we hope can help.

Getting Started

Planning for repatriation is an intense process, and there are a couple of early steps you can take to help set yourself up for success.

Preliminary Research

Before you bring this initiative to your greater community, we recommend you do some preliminary research on where and what type of heritage from your community or Nation's territory is held in museums. Starting this research in your own backyard is a great idea, as several institutions in BC are actively working in repatriation. Part 3: Conducting Research provides more detail on how to conduct this research. Part 4: Repatriation from the Royal BC Museum provides information about the Royal BC Museum and its approaches to repatriation; it also provides a link to our searchable online database. To research other museums in BC and beyond, see Appendix G: Global Museums with Major Indigenous Collections from BC.

Community Engagement: Bringing the Community Together

Repatriation involves the whole community, so a great place to start is by bringing people together to learn and talk about repatriation. Community engagement has proven very effective in advancing the work of repatriation. Whether a community is just starting out or is 40 years in, it is important to keep everyone informed and on the same page. In preparing for a meeting, three key questions are:

1. What do you want to achieve at the meeting?
2. What information do people need to know in order to be effective participants?
3. How can this information be provided in an informative, accessible manner?

Checklist for a Successful Repatriation Meeting

1. Advertise well in advance.
2. Ensure Elders are aware of the meeting.
3. Create an agenda.
4. Assign a facilitator or chairperson.
5. Assign a minute-taker.
6. Prepare an information package that people can take home with them; make sure the text and images are big enough for Elders to read.
7. Ensure the meeting space is organized so Elders can hear properly.
8. Check if Elders need rides to and from the meeting.
9. Have refreshments!

Getting Your House in Order: Building an Organizational Structure

Developing an organizational structure and operating procedures will keep the work of repatriation grounded, focused and accountable. Organizational structures define roles, responsibilities and the governance required to achieve a collective goal, and they are very helpful in the work of repatriation. When creating an organizational structure, consider the tasks outlined in this section.

Finding People to Do the Work

Who will be tasked with the work? Do you have an organization in the community that can take this work on, or do you need to create a new one? Will staff need to be hired, or is this something that can be incorporated into existing workloads? Some responsibilities required to do the work of repatriation are:

- Administration
- Planning and coordination
- Reporting
- Grant writing and fundraising
- Research
- Communications
- Community engagement and consultations
- Liaising and negotiating with museums

Establishing a Repatriation Committee

Committees are often established to help accomplish a specific goal. They are often composed of members who have experience or knowledge that will help contribute to the work of the committee and, ultimately, help the committee achieve its goals.

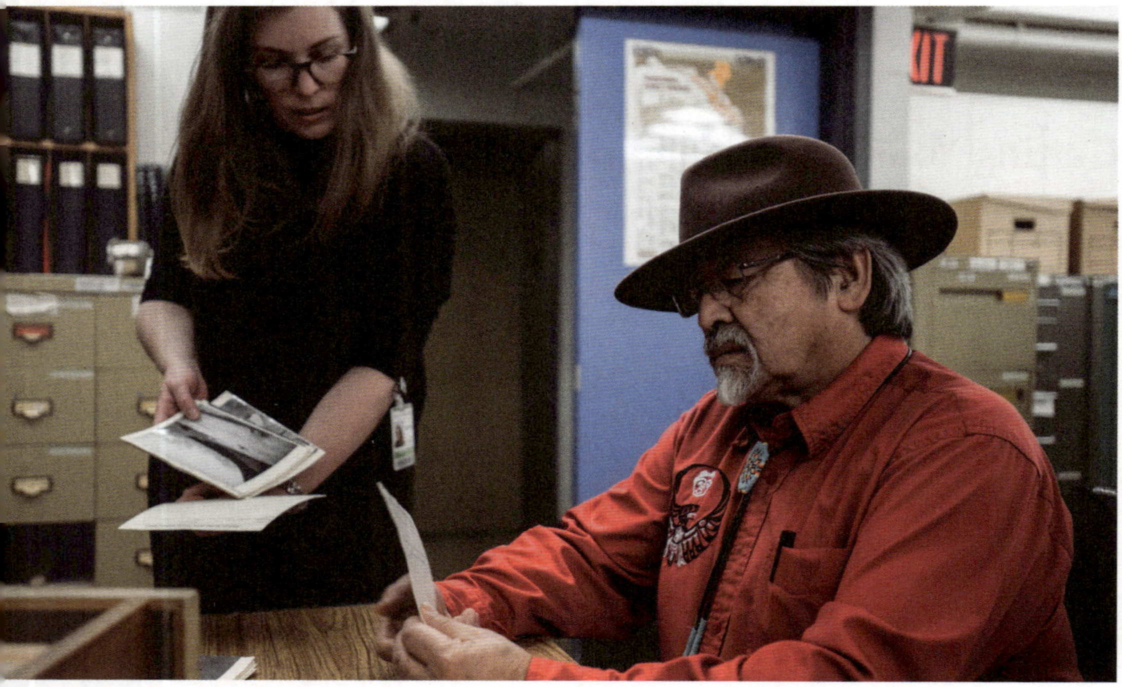

Anthropology collections manager and researcher Dr. Genevieve Hill looking at photos with Indigenous Advisory and Advocacy Committee member Dr. Ron Ignace.

Once an official body has been designated to do the work of repatriation, they will require a formal document from the leaders of their community or Nation that affirms this designation. Both museums and communities/Nations need this information to avoid potential conflicts around claims or returns and to ensure accountability.

Developing a Mandate, Vision and Guiding Principles for the Committee

As part of the process of establishing a repatriation committee (or any community group or organization), it is helpful to begin by inviting community members together to share ideas and perspectives on why it is important for a committee or group to be formed.

At such a meeting, community feedback, ideas and perspectives are gathered, and similar statements can be grouped together and added to the sample in Appendix C: Organizational Templates, Procedures and Examples. Our sample can be customized to replace headings with new ones that reflect the community's and committee's intent.

> ***I had no idea of the journey that I would go on, no idea that it would be a lifelong journey to help my Ancestors. I brought that message home to my community, and people were called to action, and we travelled the world looking for our Ancestors.***
>
> ~ Lucy Bell, Head of the Indigenous Collections and Repatriation Department, Royal BC Museum

Creating a Terms of Reference Document

As part of the process of establishing an organization or other body to do the work of repatriation, it is helpful to begin by inviting community members together to share ideas and perspectives on why it is important for a committee or group to be formed. A terms of reference document outlines how a group has agreed to work together, its values and principles, and its goals. Community feedback, ideas and perspectives are critical to keeping everyone on track moving forward together.

Once the work of developing initial statements about the committee's vision, mission and mandate is done, a committee terms of reference document can now be developed. The terms of reference provide clear parameters and direction around the committee's goals, scope of authority, and their role in the process of repatriation. These are the main elements of a terms of reference document:

- Goals
- Members
- Roles
- Meetings
- Scope of authority
- Budget
- Structure
- Purpose
- Responsibilities
- Decision-making process
- Reporting requirements
- Deliverables

Most terms of reference documents begin with an introduction section to explain the reason for establishing the committee, and a background section that explains where the committee is positioned within the organization or community that is establishing the committee. For a sample terms of reference document, see Appendix C: Organizational Templates, Procedures and Examples.

Setting Timelines and Budgets

No matter how big or small your repatriation projects are, it is important to create your work plan and budget. For examples of both, see Appendix C: Organizational Templates, Procedures and Examples.

Putting Out Calls for Proposals

When your project needs professional services, you may wish to reach out to potential contractors through a call or request for proposals. A call or request for proposals is the same thing: an invitation for professionals (from independent businesses, artists, or contractors to large companies) to respond to a need your organization has expressed, and to provide a bid, quote for service, proposal or prospectus that demonstrates their ability to address the needs of the organization. For a sample call for proposals, see Appendix C: Organizational Templates, Procedures and Examples.

Fundraising

Repatriation costs both time and money: for research; organization and community consultations; reburial preparations; travel and transport; the creation of museums, cultural centres and archives, etc. The true cost depends on each Indigenous Nation's approach to repatriation. Sometimes mainstream museums have a budget, or can provide in-kind support toward expenses incurred by Indigenous Nations in bringing their Ancestors home. It depends on the museum, so don't be afraid to ask what they can contribute.

In 2017, the Royal BC Museum launched the first grant in Canada created specifically for repatriation. The Canadian government is expected to eventually do the same. Many granting agencies already understand that repatriation is a necessary part of reconciliation and healing.

Appendix D: Fundraising Resources lists some of the organizations that fund arts and heritage projects that can support repatriation, even if they are not designed specifically for this work. Be creative: you can apply grants toward travel, art projects, internships, professional development, research, language revitalization, etc. When applying for grants, contact funding officers ahead of time so they can help guide you in writing your grant, and make sure to read the grant-writing tips in Appendix D: Fundraising Resources. As well, don't forget to look into corporate and private foundation grants.

Grants can cover many costs, and most mainstream museums might have a small budget to contribute as well. Another way to help cover costs is community fundraising. Loonie / toonie auctions, raffles, fundraising dinners, GoFundMe campaigns, selling merchandise and getting donation jars out can be other ways to create financial resources for repatriation.

Returning remains to their communities can create financial demands on some of the most impoverished communities in our country. Some may think, what do they need all that money for? I would suggest you recall or imagine arranging a funeral for one of your loved ones. Everything adds up: the cost of the undertaker, the casket, the flowers, the lunch or tea afterwards, the newspaper obituary. In our communities, the wrappers, the diggers, the singers, the cooks, the meals, the blankets. Funerals cost money. Repatriation and reburials of human remains are funerals in every sense.

~ Dianne Hinkley, Cowichan Tribes

Working with Other Communities

The work of repatriation involves many parties, which means that sometimes needs and priorities can conflict. It's important to think about your neighbours, as well as the needs of the people on whose territory you'll be working when at mainstream museums.

Overlapping Territories and Individual Community Needs

If there are overlapping territories or different communities with different needs within your greater Nation, consider how you are going work together. For example, some museum records only list the region, and not the community, from which an Ancestor or cultural belonging originated; how will you and your neighbours address this? This is a very important consideration for a community and/or Nation's repatriation process, and for a museum's ability to repatriate to the "right" community or Nation without conflict or error. Contact your neighbours to advise them of your plans; see if there is a need or want for joint community consultations, planning or the repatriation itself. If there is a partnership, it is a good idea to have this arrangement incorporated into your organizational structure and terms of reference. See Part 7: Case Study: Repatriation Journey of the Haida Nation for an example.

Protocols for Acknowledging Indigenous Territories and Their Peoples

In some cases, the museum you're working with will be located on the land of a different Indigenous People. Indigenous protocols

Amelia Rea carries Haida Ancestral remains to their final resting place.

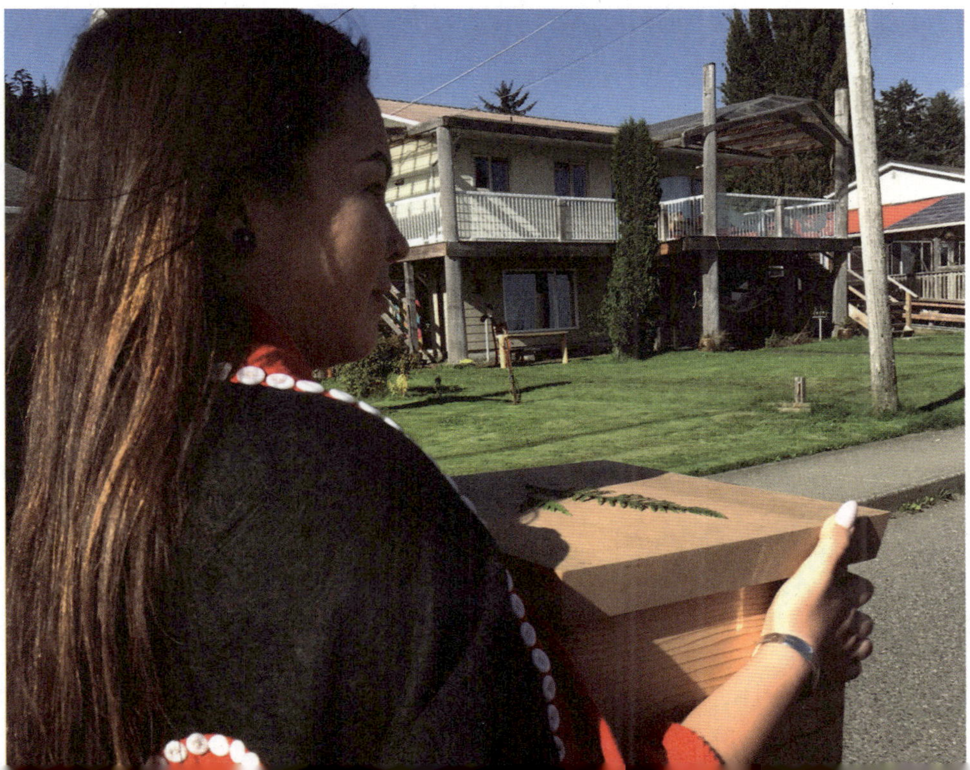

generally require that when someone from one Indigenous Nation travels into the territory of another Nation, the people meet to conduct business (i.e., land acknowledgements from the visiting Nation; a welcome from the host Nation) and for cultural exchange. Some museums have worked with Indigenous communities for a long time and have established working relationships and protocols with them. Others may have just started. Not every museum in North America has a connection with the Indigenous Nation on whose territory their institution sits. Ask the museum to connect you with their host Nation. If they don't know who this is, it is a great opportunity for them to find out! You may wish to bring along gifts or other items appropriate for culture-sharing with your host Nation.

We all want the best for the Ancestral remains. So, the issue of overlapping interests may be a cursory detail we have to work through. But again, if we identify the main goal, if we keep our eyes on the prize at the end, which is the respectful treatment of the Ancestors, then I'm sure this step becomes much less of an onerous task.

~ Dr. Genevieve Hill, Royal BC Museum Anthropology Collections Manager and Researcher

Spiritual and Emotional Considerations

It's easy to get caught up in the logistics of the repatriation process, but it's very important to take care of your spiritual and mental well-being as well.

When Things Get Emotional

This is an important topic that should be discussed and explored at home before getting too deep into the work. To get an idea of other Indigenous experiences in repatriation, check out the success stories in Appendix J: Repatriation Success Stories and the case study in Part 7: Case Study: Repatriation Journey of the Haida Nation. When you consider how most Indigenous Ancestors and belongings left their homelands, it is pretty hard not to get emotional, and this can happen at any time during the process: during meetings, while researching or planning, and especially when you go to museums to visit your cultural belongings or bring your Ancestors and heritage home.

Anger and grief often rise to the surface, but so do hope and joy, as work progresses and reparations are made. People who have done this work for years still struggle with anger and grief at times, though it does

Community members Jeanette Jules and Dalton Silver in the ethnology collection area.

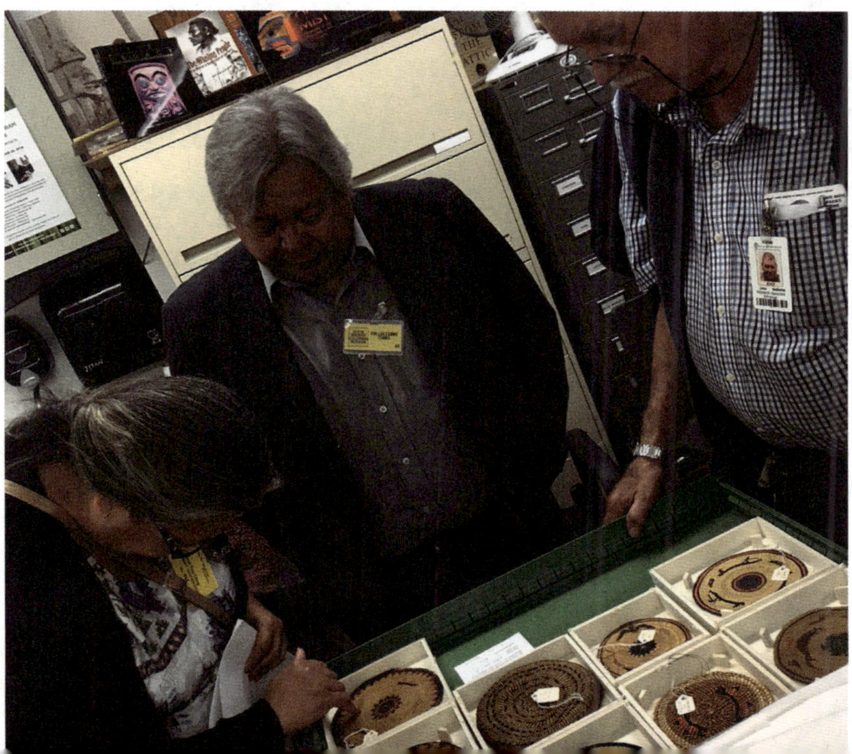

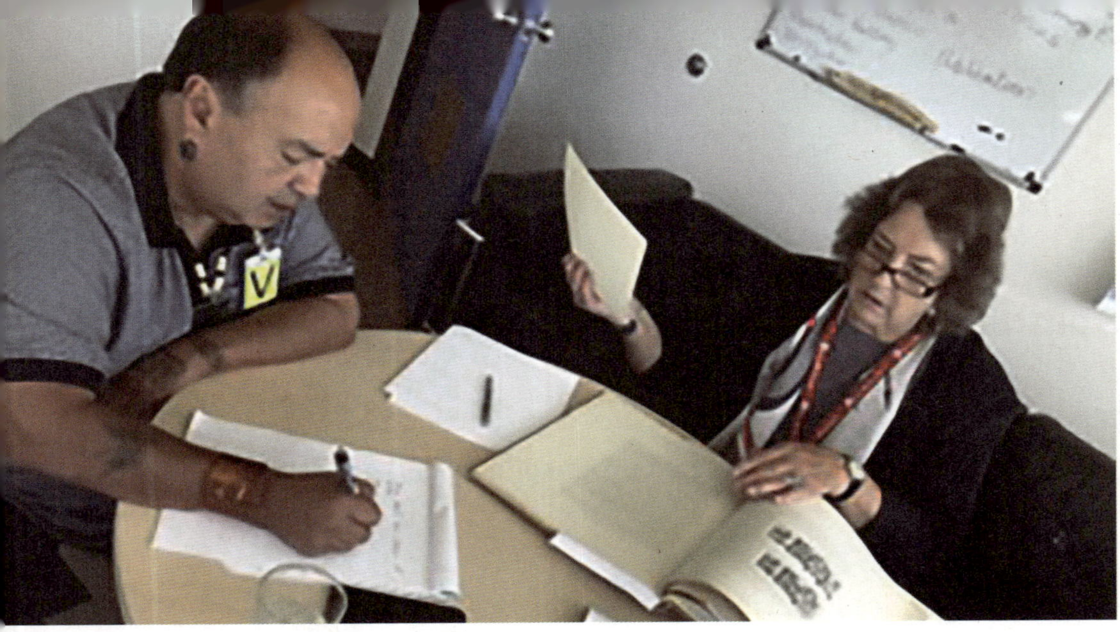

Willie White and Martha Black curating the weaving display.

get a bit easier as you go along. Many Nations have found repatriation to be a great healer, especially when bringing their Ancestors home.

It is a good idea to put support systems in place, both in the community and during visits to these museums. There are many different types of support systems, and which you set up will depend on what works best for the person or people in need. Some ideas around emotional and spiritual support can come in the form of spiritual and medicinal practitioners in your community, people in your community or from other Nations who've gone through the same experience, the strength of Elders and the love and innocence of children, counselling, getting out on the land, and cleansing in rivers or the ocean.

When I'm bringing my students to the museums, I have a meeting with them, to come together with a good heart before we go into the vaults, because they have to understand that our people are going to greet us as soon as we walk in that door. I really believe that our people are standing right beside me; they're calling me, "Come here! Come look at me! Don't go over there! You don't want to look at that robe, you want to look at me over here."

~ Willie White, Tsimshian Nation, weaver

Spiritual and Ceremonial Practices

Each Nation has its own beliefs and practices. Explore this in your community and, if you like, with other Nations. What we can say here is that museums must provide space and understanding for Indigenous people to practise our ways. Many museums now have smudge rooms or outdoor areas for food burnings. Some of the stories about how museums got to this place are pretty interesting, and even comical (this brings to light another good tip: bring some good Indigenous humour with you, because you will need it at times!). The responsibility Indigenous people hold here is to clearly communicate their needs to museums well in advance of a visit to ensure these institutions aren't blindsided. This also provides time to problem-solve if there are challenges for the museum in meeting these requirements.

A teenager told me that his grandmother told him that they were going to the hall for the return-home ceremony of T'xwelátse. The teen told me that he didn't want to go, but his grandma told him that he didn't have a choice, he had to go. At the ceremony, when he first saw our Ancestor, he realized that he didn't know that he had a hole in his heart at the same moment he knew that he was healed.

~ David Schaepe, Director and Senior Archaeologist for the Stó:lō Research and Resource Management Centre

Getting Experience in the Fields of Indigenous Language, Arts, Culture, Heritage and Museology

The phrase "Indigenous scholarship" might make one think of an Indigenous person who has achieved Western academic credentials—and it does. Indigenous scholarship also refers to Nation-based learning: gaining an education and training from the knowledge-holders and culture-keepers in your community. Elders, language speakers, artists, historians, food gatherers and preparers, mariners, medicinal and spiritual practitioners, and many others involved in specialized fields carry foundational cultural knowledge and practices that can help to empower the work of repatriation and Indigenous museology.

Combining this knowledge with educational programs and hands-on training gained from organizations working in Indigenous language, arts, culture, heritage and history is a home run! Participating in these types of educational and training programs is a great way to learn about arts administration, curation, educational programming and publication development, as well as archives, collections and cultural resource management, among other things. Some great opportunities for engaging in this learning are provided in Appendix H: Resources on Education in Indigenous Museology. Some programs have post-secondary requirements; others do not.

Working in a museum, archive or cultural centre is an amazing way to both care for your heritage and learn about how these institutions work. Some who have participated in programs, co-op positions or internships have gone on to find good jobs in the fields of language, arts, culture and heritage—in their own communities and in mainstream institutions. Getting Indigenous people "into the system" also helps to Indigenize mainstream institutions.

For example, many Indigenous participants in the Aboriginal Cultural Stewardship Program administered by the First Peoples' Cultural

Council, Royal BC Museum and University of Victoria in the 1990s went on to work in museums and cultural centres throughout North America.

I was fortunate that I got selected to be one of the visiting artist researchers through the Bill Holm Foundation. This was really exciting for me, because I had never actually had my hands on one of those poles, and it was so exciting to be able to put my hands on that, feel where all the designs were, the depths of the cuts, the angle of the cuts and those kinds of things that we look for as artists is that style and those techniques.

~ Lou-ann Neel, Royal BC Museum Repatriation Specialist

Betty Richardson and Genevieve Weber looking at archival materials.

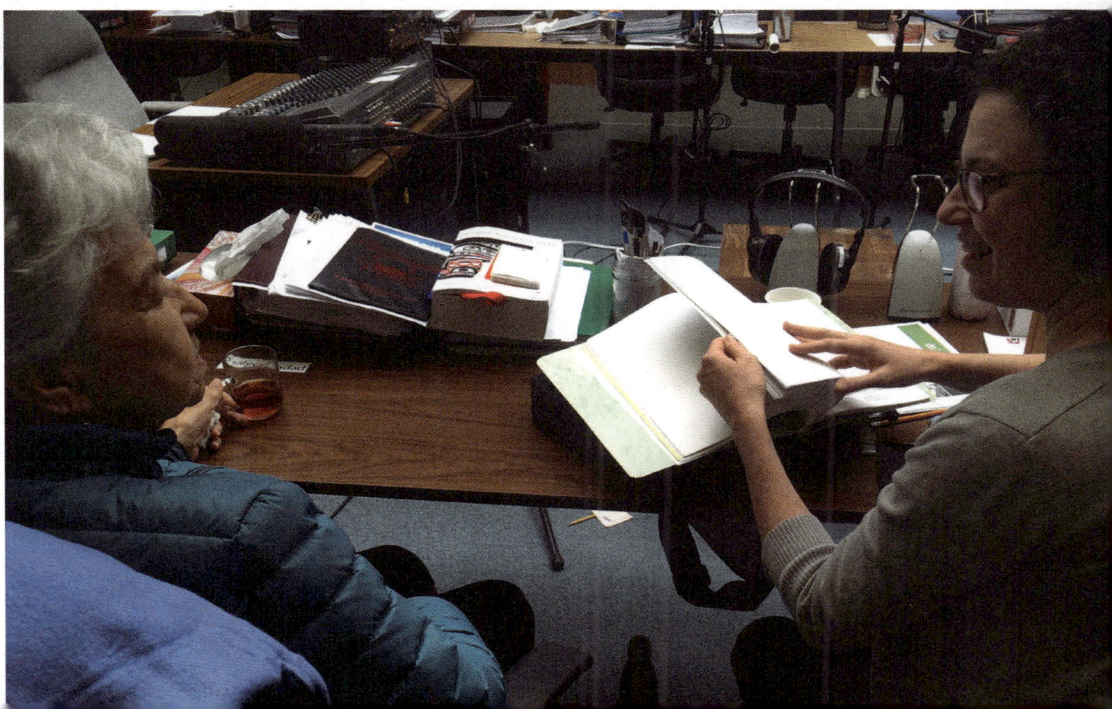

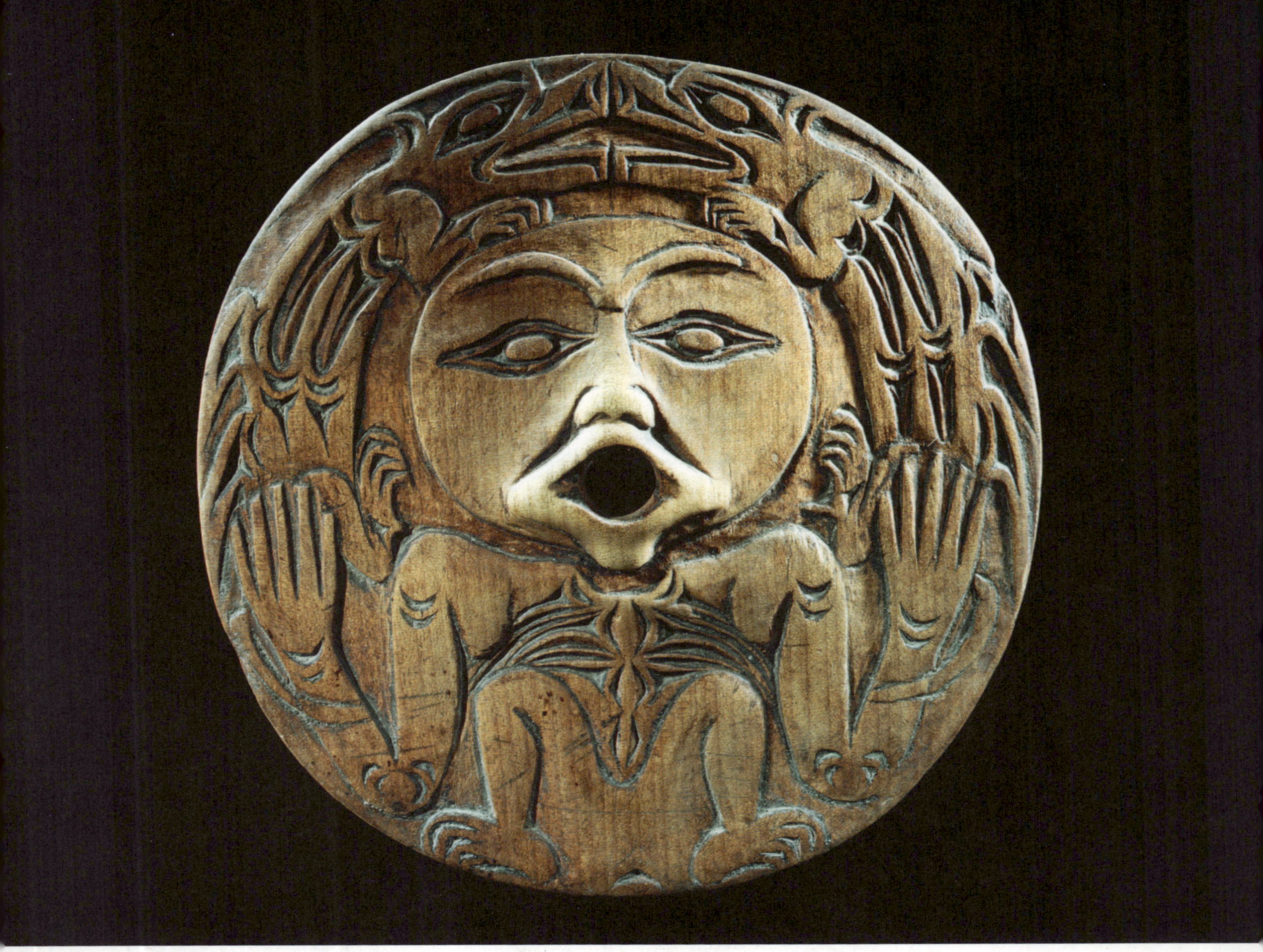

Coast Salish spindle whorl, ethnology collections, RBCM 2454.

PART 3

Conducting Research

Repatriation research can be quite an intensive and long-term process, and very exciting, too. This section provides some research tips that may help your repatriation journey.

Arming Yourself with Knowledge

Part 2: Organizing a Successful Repatriation provides an overview of how Indigenous Ancestors and belongings wound up in museums, universities and private collections around the world. Today in North America, there are museum and gallery people who have experience working with Indigenous communities in repatriation. Many of these people and other staff in museums know this history to a good degree and are quite easy to work with. But there are many who might just be starting out in repatriation from the museum side, with little or no experience, or maybe they don't know the true history of Indigenous

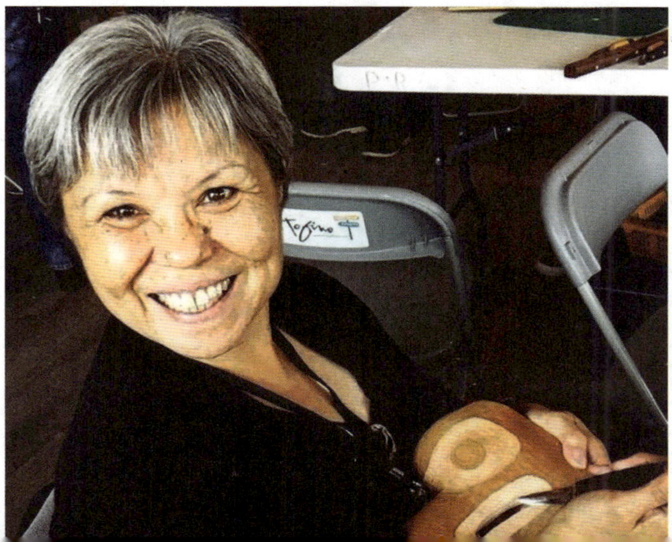

Lou-ann Neel, Kwakwa̲ka̲'wakw artist.

Nations and Canada. In other parts of the world, some people may have never met an Indigenous person from North America before.

Being well versed on the timeline and impact of Canadian colonial regimes on Indigenous people in general, as well as your own Nation's personal experience from this period, can be very useful in both educating people in museums and in repatriation negotiations. Find out what knowledge exists in your community about the era of colonial collecting, and check out the following resources that explore the history of Indigenous people and Canada:

- Union of BC Indian Chiefs historical timeline
  ubcic.bc.ca/timeline
- UBC Indigenous Foundations
  indigenousfoundations.arts.ubc.ca/home
- BC Archives
  search-bcarchives.royalbcmuseum.bc.ca

Finding Your Ancestors and Cultural Heritage

Finding your Ancestors is a big and very interesting job. The Ancestors and cultural heritage of Indigenous people in BC are scattered around the world. Appendix G: Global Museums with Major Indigenous Collections from BC provides links to a number of museums and the collections they house, but keep in mind that this list is far from

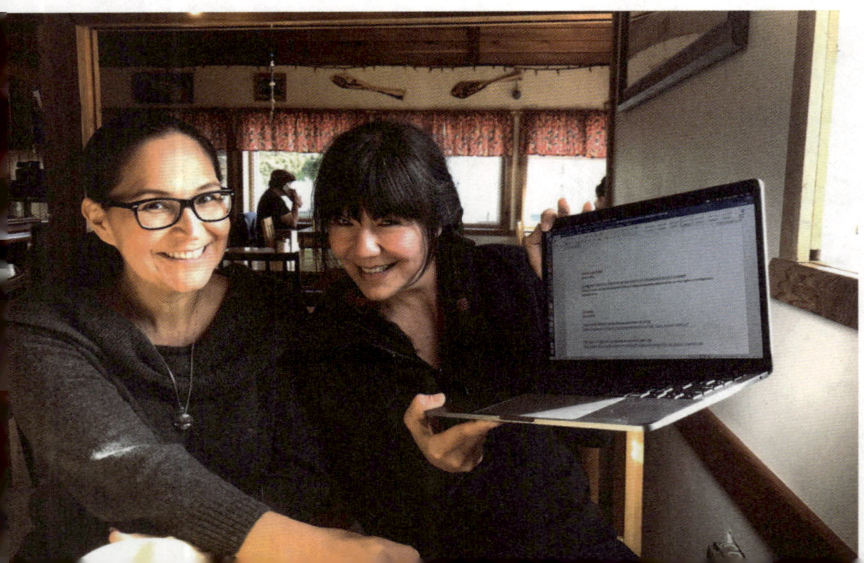

Lucy Bell, head of the Indigenous Collections and Repatriation Department, and Nika Collison, executive director and curator at the Haida Gwaii Museum at K̲ay Llnagaay, working on the repatriation handbook.

complete! Information on more museums will be added in revised editions of this handbook. There are several ways to do this research: online, in your community and on site at museums and archives.

Online Research

Searching online databases can be fun, but if you are new to this type of research, it can feel intimidating. Sometimes it is as easy as typing your Nation or community's name into the collections search engine. Other times it can be more complex, but doable. Sometimes there are directions for navigating the searches directly on the website, or maybe there's a computer whiz around who can help you. There might be an email address on the website that you can use to contact someone for help. If not, try contacting the museum's collections department for assistance. If you are able to get into the site and start searching, but nothing is coming up, try a few different ways of spelling your Nation's name.

A handy resource to start finding where your treasures might be is the UBC Reciprocal Research Network, which provides information on and images of Indigenous cultural items held at dozens of institutions. It is a great place to get to get an idea of what might be out there! www.rrncommunity.org

Often online collections do not represent the complete collection held in a museum, or may not provide online information about Ancestral remains out of sensitivity. In addition, treasures held in museums might have been misattributed to other regions or Nations, so take the time to search other collections as well.

Some museums may not have collections available online, period. After checking out a museum's website, contact its collections department and ask for a complete inventory of Ancestral remains and cultural heritage originating in, or attributed to, your territory.

Don't forget about archives: some of the main collectors took field notes or photographs that may or may not be included with the catalogue records. Sometimes this information winds up in a different department of the institution, or a different institution altogether. Ask the museum people about this—they can often send you in the right direction.

Community Research

The scholarship that exists within Indigenous communities is stunning, especially so considering the impacts of colonization. It is amazing what can happen on many levels when a community can access and take care of their Ancestors and belongings, including the sharing of knowledge. There are many people to involve in community research: Elders, artists, historians, language speakers, researchers, medicinal and spiritual practitioners, canoe-makers, big-house builders, food gatherers and preparers, those reborn and many more. Those not working in a specialized field, or who have not had much chance for cultural training, bring a lot to the table, too. People who are starting out in their learning ask questions or have insights that can lead to information and ideas that have not yet been considered.

On-site Museum Research

Each community will do what works best for them, but following are some ideas to consider when doing your research at a museum. For specific information about research at the Royal BC Museum, see Part 4: Repatriation from the Royal BC Museum.

Preliminary Research

Twenty years ago, it was barely possible to research Indigenous collections online, but today, many museums have made collections searchable on their websites. These sites are very handy in getting an idea of what is out there. Keep in mind that when a museum puts collections online, sometimes it's not the whole collection, even if what is made available seems like a lot. Contact these museums and request a full inventory of your heritage held in their institutions.

The work of repatriation is ongoing, so it is not always necessary to locate every piece before meeting with your community. For example, the Haida have been locating and researching their heritage held in museums for decades, and this process is still ongoing. Once you've located some museums that hold your heritage, you can bring this information to people for community research and guidance. Once community members have identified priority museums, arrange for a research and relationship-building visit ... and a repatriation, if things progress quickly. See Appendix E: Sample Letters to Museums for examples of letters to museums to arrange for access to collections and help with locating objects, as well as a sample repatriation request.

On-site Research

In planning your travels, if you haven't already, request a printed and digital copy of records on your treasures held in the museum, so your community can familiarize themselves with what they will see. In addition to the possibility that not everything is available on a museum's website, having to go online over and over isn't always the easiest or most practical for remote communities with slow internet; downloading images and records from websites and organizing them can be *very* time consuming.

Museums tend to categorize objects by the artistic style or technologies attributed to Indigenous Nations or communities. Be prepared for the possibility of incorrect attributions when researching your heritage; for example, the museum's catalogue records might say a piece is "Haida," but it might actually be of Tsimshian manufacture, or vice versa.

During the height of colonial collecting, some collectors were not that great at documenting where pieces were acquired from, or which Nation they were associated with, or they may have acquired them in another Nation's territory, or from another collector. Or maybe a work came in with no information, and museums assigned attributions that also may or may not have been correct. The reasons go on and on. Great numbers of treasures are also unattributed: they may just say "Northwest Coast" or assign a couple of attributions based on regional styles of art and technologies, such as "Northwest Coast, Tlingit or Haida."

It is emotional to visit your Ancestors and cultural heritage in museums. It can be weird or upsetting if you are not used to visiting museums and their storage areas, or if you are experiencing mainstream museum practices for the first time, even if museums are working to Indigenize their practices. For some tips on preparing for your emotional, psychological, and spiritual safety and health, see Spiritual and Emotional Considerations (page 23).

It can be overwhelming to travel to new places, and expensive—especially when travelling to big cities. There are a lot of logistics to figure out when planning a trip to a museum. For some tips, see Appendix F: Tips for Planning for Travel and Transport.

Bring a camera to document your cultural belongings: museums don't always have or make available images of various angles of an object, digital photos can be low resolution, and you might want close-up photos of certain elements on a piece. Keeping track of catalogue numbers associated with your photographs can be challenging, but is necessary for future reference. A great way to keep track is to take a photo of the catalogue number before you take photos of the piece itself, or have a notepad and write the numbers down in the order that you take photos. Then you can organize your research when you get home. Consider photo-documenting your trip for community records, and if possible, film your experiences as well.

These visits are opportune times to get to know museum staff and provide advice on proper storage and handling of your Ancestors and belongings before they come home, or for those pieces of cultural heritage that might stay. Speaking of museum people, it is common for staff to take notes, request oral history interviews, or photograph or videotape your visit.

Intellectual Property Rights

Protect your intellectual property rights! Old-school colonial research methods dictate that the collector maintains copyright to their "research" (your knowledge and words, photographs and video of you, etc.). This means the institution and other researchers can do with it as they please; sometimes it also means that you have to get permission to use the information you shared with them or be able to use imagery or video footage. Colonial collecting is so yesterday! Many museums are changing these practices, but make sure to review your release form. See Appendix C: Organizational Templates, Procedures and Examples for an example of a release form the Haida Gwaii Museum uses when conducting research in our community, and with others, which is designed to ensure the person who has shared their knowledge maintains their intellectual property rights.

Creating Relationships with Museum People: The Art of Indigenous Diplomacy

When museums and Indigenous people work together with respect, it can lead to mutually beneficial, long-term relationships. Relationships are important for so many reasons, but given the history of how Indigenous Ancestors and cultural heritage wound up in global institutions, sometimes it can be hard to bring diplomacy to the work of repatriation. As well, some museum people may have no experience in repatriation and can take a while to make a connection.

You will find that many museum people are delightful human beings. Some may even be repatriation-ready! Some museum staff carry settler guilt, or shame about their institution's colonial history or their own settler history, and are working hard to make change in themselves and the institutions they work in—but the people working in museums today are not the ones who put Indigenous Ancestral remains and cultural heritage into their institutions. The real shame would be if they refused to work with Indigenous Peoples. Thankfully, this old-school way has changed in many institutions, and it will continue to do so in other museums.

Some institutions are ready to work together, and some can work on a repatriation process quite quickly. For example, the Royal BC Museum has created a very efficient process for the repatriation of Ancestral remains. Other institutions might be more resistant in the beginning if they do not have experience in repatriation or in working with Indigenous people in general. Indigenous diplomacy has been critical in opening doors for the Indigenous repatriation movement and in changing colonial museum practices.

Relationship-building can bring so much to the repatriation process, and for the reparation and healing that comes with doing this work. You may also wish to share some of your traditional beliefs with the museum staff. Museum people are often eager to learn about Indigenous people and their cultures. Take this opportunity to educate staff on the collections that are in their care, for example, by providing parameters or guidance around culturally appropriate management of your collections through considerations such as public access, handling and storage. Consider involving museum people in some of your ceremonies, if appropriate. Cultural sharing is a powerful act that can change perspectives, strengthen spirits and make the work of repatriation that much easier. It's a great way to build relationships and to celebrate with the staff, as they are on this repatriation and reconciliation journey, too.

Emotional and Spiritual Preparation

It is so important to prepare people before they head off to museums to research or repatriate. Mainstream museums and practices can be incredibly foreign to many Indigenous people. As discussed in Part 2: Organizing a Successful Repatriation, the work of repatriation can be highly emotional, especially when people visit their Ancestors and cultural belongings held in storage, or even on display, or if they find an Ancestor or treasure related to their lineage. It can be an especially delicate time when preparing Ancestors for their journey home.

There is great need to prepare travellers for what they might expect. Experience has proven it is important for the delegation to be grounded in traditional beliefs and practices ahead of time, and to have the process for preparing their Ancestors for the journey home well thought out. If you are going on a repatriation trip for the first time, contact another Nation with experience in repatriation, and check out the resources provided in Appendix F: Tips for Planning for Travel and Transport.

> ***Relationships are the key, in our experience, to have space for dialogue, to get together, to connect and to maintain those relationships through time.***
>
> ~ David Schaepe, Director and Senior Archaeologist for the Stó:lō Research and Resource Management Centre

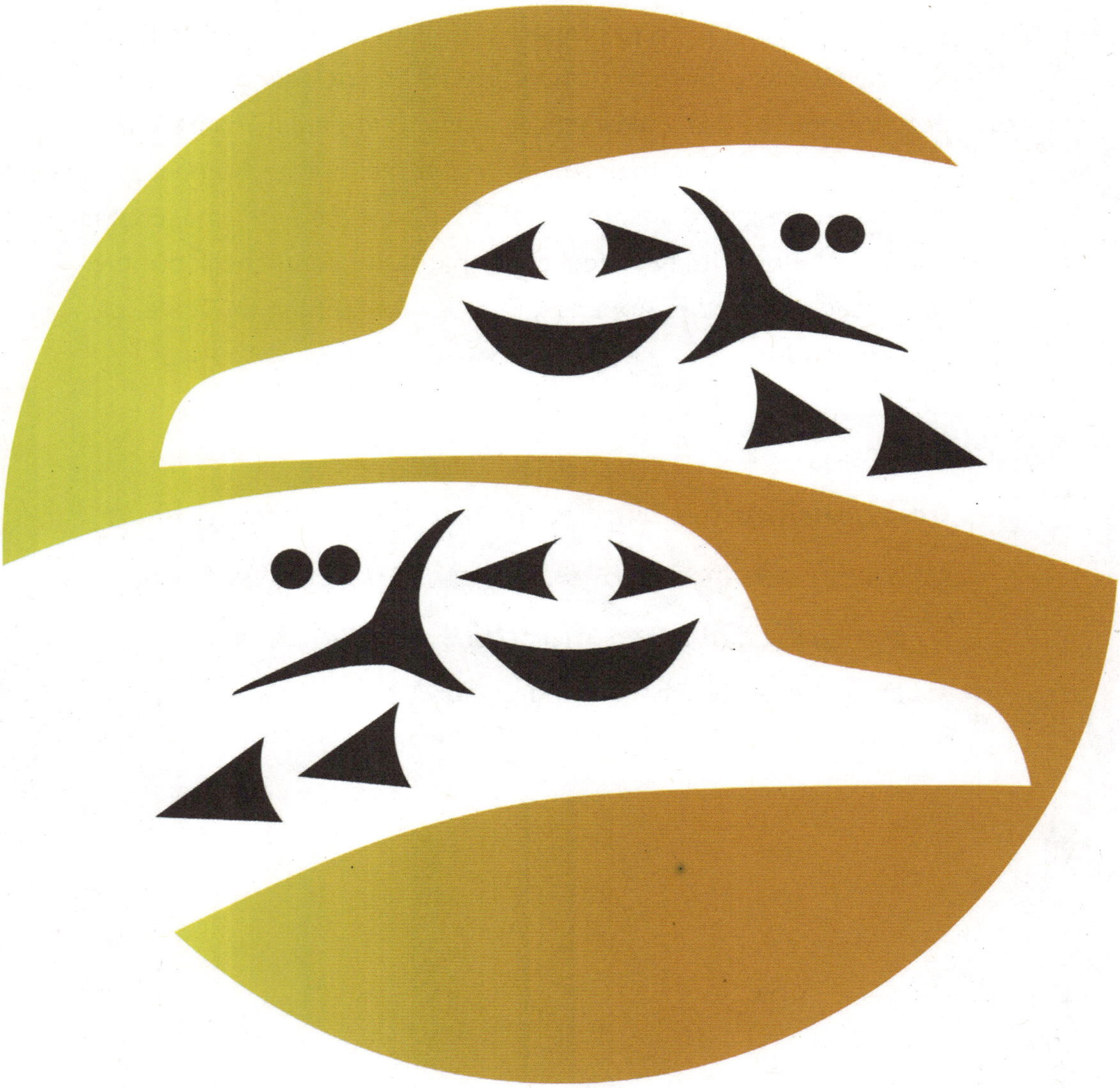

PART 4
Repatriation from the Royal BC Museum

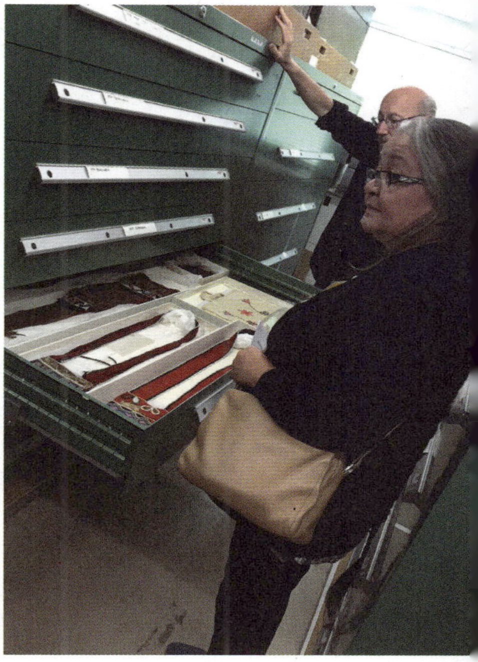

Jeanette Jules and Brian Seymour, anthropology collections manager.

The Royal BC Museum and the BC Archives together make up the Royal BC Museum Corporation, located on the traditional territories of the Lekwungen Peoples. At the museum and archives, we are committed to meaningful and respectful relationships and partnerships with Indigenous Nations, co-management and physical and digital repatriation of cultural materials, the return of Ancestral remains, and the implementation of the Truth and Reconciliation Commission's Calls to Action. See Appendix I: Frequently Asked Questions about Repatriation for FAQs about repatriation from the Royal BC Museum.

Indigenous Collections and Repatriation Department

The Indigenous Collections and Repatriation Department at the Royal BC Museum is committed to caring for the thousands of invaluable Indigenous items we have the honour of housing, and we are equally committed to the work of repatriation in line with the recommendations of the Truth and Reconciliation Commission.

Indigenous Collections and Repatriation Policy

The Indigenous collections in the museum and archives are guided by the Royal BC Museum's Indigenous Collections and Repatriation Policy: rbcm.ca/first-nations/first-nations-repatriation
The policy also guides our repatriation activities.

Indigenous Repatriation Symposium

In April 2017 the Royal BC Museum, in partnership with the First Peoples' Cultural Council, hosted the Indigenous Perspectives on Repatriation: Moving Forward Together symposium. Feedback from participants provided the Indigenous Collections and Repatriation Department with recommendations that helped inform the department's strategic plan, and a range of action items that could be implemented soon after the symposium. The wise words of the symposium speakers are found within the handbook. Details of these recommendations can be found here: rbcm.ca/collections/first-nations/repatriation/symposium

Indigenous Advisory and Advocacy Committee

The Indigenous Advisory and Advocacy Committee (IAAC) was established in 2017 to "advise the Museum on effective and respectful engagement with Indigenous communities on matters relating to the Museum's governance, corporate planning, operations and repatriation. IAAC also plays an important advocacy role for the Museum and for the Indigenous Peoples of BC."

IAAC is composed of Indigenous community members with expertise across a range of areas of interest to Indigenous communities in British Columbia, with a particular focus on tangible and intangible cultural heritage, repatriation, cultural interpretation and education. More information about IAAC can be found by searching the Royal BC Museum's website.

Strategic Plan

The 2019–2022 strategic plan for the Indigenous Collections and Repatriation Department provides greater detail on the mission, values, guiding principles, strategies and specific actions the department will undertake over the next three years to support the museum's broader mandates and vision. The strategic plan can be viewed online at the Royal BC Museum's website.

Researching Indigenous Collections at the Royal BC Museum and Archives

At the Royal BC Museum, you can access extensive and diverse resources related to the cultures and histories of Indigenous communities, families and individuals in BC.

These resources include objects of tangible and intangible heritage: cultural objects and regalia, artifacts and belongings, historical photographs, audio and visual recordings, documents and more. They can be viewed in the exhibitions, and also by scheduling visits to the many collections that are not on display.

The rest of this section outlines the collections in the museum and archives, how they can be accessed online and in person, and whom to contact for advice and assistance. We invite you to visit the museum's website to get started (see the First Nations section and the BC Archives section). For more help, please contact any of the people listed on page 45.

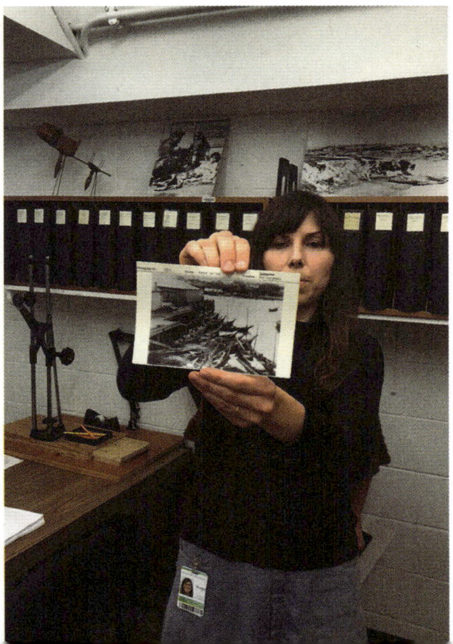

Brooke Albers, audiovisual collections manager, with ethnology photo card.

Table 1.
Overview of RBCM collections and BC Archives records.

RBCM Indigenous Collections and Repatriation Department			BC Archives	
Indigenous Collection	Audiovisual Collection	Archaeology Collection	Government Records	Private Records
Over 15,000 historical and modern cultural objects and related documentation	Over 20,000 photographs, field notes, over 3,000 audio recordings and transcriptions	Over 215,000 artifacts and cultural materials, field records and photographs, maps, faunal material and soil samples, petroglyph rubbings, Ancestral remains[4]	Provincial and colonial government records	Private, community and business records, which include paintings, photographs, maps, publications, correspondence, diaries, and sound and film recordings

Royal BC Museum Collections

The Royal BC Museum Indigenous collections are cared for by the Indigenous Collections and Repatriation Department. Staff members in this department and their contact information are listed on page 45.

Indigenous Collection

The ethnology collection consists of approximately 15,000 cultural objects from Indigenous cultures and communities across the province, as well as related documentation. It contains both historical and modern cultural materials of many kinds, including regalia and ceremonial items, textiles, domestic utensils, traditional clothing, carvings, basketry, prints and other artworks. This extensive collection can be searched online at: search-collections.royalbcmuseum.bc.ca/ethnology

4 Note that Ancestral remains are not actually part of the museum's collections, as they have not been accessioned.

For more information about the collection, for assistance using the database, or to schedule a visit to the collection, please contact Brian Seymour, collections manager, anthropology (bseymour@royalbcmuseum.bc.ca).

Audiovisual Collection

The audiovisual collection is part of the ethnology collection. It consists of photographs, audio recordings, films, videos and related documentation. In the spirit of reconciliation, the Royal BC Museum now waives the processing fees for private Indigenous researchers to receive copies of intangible heritage, although it may take a while to distribute the resources due to high demand.

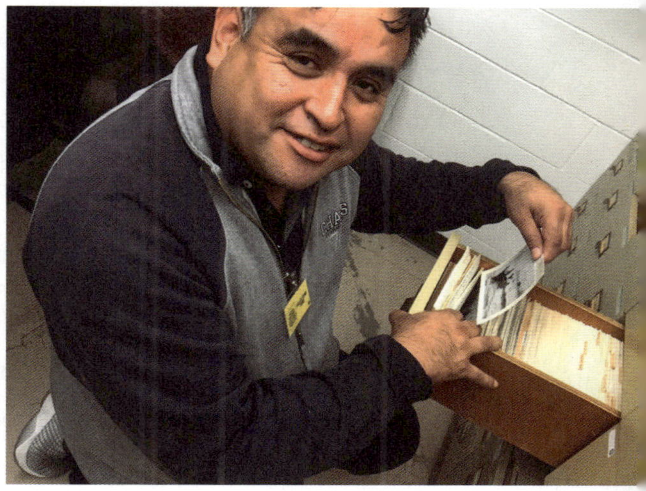

Nathan Charlie, Ahousaht First Nation, viewing ethnology collection photo card drawer.

Photographs

The photograph collection contains more than 65,000 images from the 19th and 20th centuries related to Indigenous Nations in and around BC. Prints on index cards are organized by community for easy viewing. The collection is not yet online, but visitors can take their own photographs of index cards and catalogue information for personal reference.

To schedule a visit, please contact one of the Indigenous Collections and Repatriation Department collection managers.

Audio Recordings

The audio recordings collection consists of approximately 3,600 recordings made between the 1950s and the present of Indigenous songs, stories, language teachings, conversations and gatherings.

For access to catalogue descriptions of the tapes, contact any of the Indigenous Collections and Repatriation Department collection managers. We will be happy to send the catalogues via email.

Once you have looked through the catalogues and identified any recordings of interest, you can listen to them at the museum by appointment, or order an mp3 or CD copy. If the recordings require written permission from the recorders, speakers or their families, we will let you know how to request this.

Films, Videos and DVDs

There are more than 125 film reels, 200 videotapes and 50 DVDs with Indigenous subject matter in the audiovisual collection. Most are available for reference only due to copyright restrictions.

For inquiries related to film, video and DVDs, contact Brooke Albers, audiovisual collections manager (balbers@royalbcmuseum.bc.ca).

Archaeology Collection

The museum holds more than 215,000 artifacts and cultural materials recovered from archaeological sites across the province, as well as field notes, photographs, maps, reports, faunal material and soil samples recovered under permit, found artifacts and Ancestral remains that were brought to the museum over the past 130 years. Most archaeological objects are stone, bone, shell or antler, but some are made from wood, plants, leather, glass or metal. The most recent date from the early 20th century; the oldest are more than 9,000 years old. In accordance with the Royal BC Museum's Indigenous Collections and Repatriation Policy, Ancestral remains are not part of the museum's collection; they are in the care of the museum until each respective First Nation is prepared to repatriate them to their home communities. Some of the collection can be searched online at search-collections.royalbcmuseum.bc.ca/Archaeology

For help searching the online catalogue, contact Dr. Genevieve Hill, collections manager and researcher, anthropology.

For inquiries regarding the repatriation of Ancestral remains, contact Dr. Genevieve Hill, or Grant Keddie, curator of archaeology.

Indigenous Collections and Repatriation Department Staff Members

Lucy Bell
Department Head
(250) 217-4522
lbell@royalbcmuseum.bc.ca

Grant Keddie
Curator, Archaeology
(250) 387-2416
gkeddie@royalbcmuseum.bc.ca

Dr. Martha Black
Curator, Ethnology
(250) 387-2457
mblack@royalbcmuseum.bc.ca

Brian Seymour
Collections Manager, Anthropology
(250) 387-2440
bseymour@royalbcmuseum.bc.ca

Dr. Genevieve Hill
Collections Manager and
Researcher, Anthropology
(250) 893-8019
ghill@royalbcmuseum.bc.ca

Sheila Sampson
Collections Assistant
(250) 387-4494
ssampson@royalbcmuseum.bc.ca

Lou-ann Neel
Repatriation Specialist
(250) 889-9674
lneel@royalbcmuseum.bc.ca

Brooke Albers
Collections Manager, Audiovisual
(778) 584-5363
balbers@royalbcmuseum.bc.ca

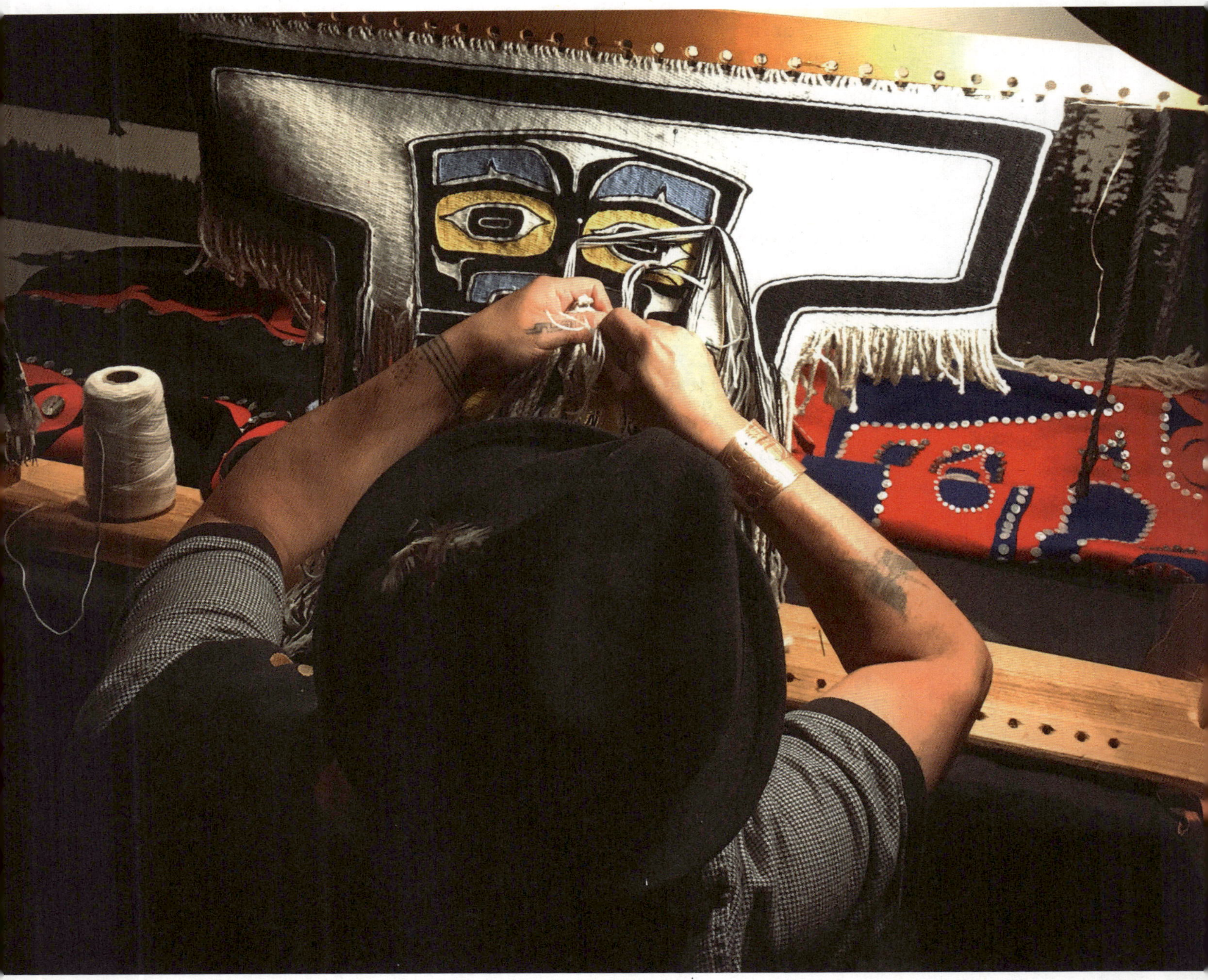

Willie White, Tsimshian weaver, creating an apron at the RBCM.

BC Archives Indigenous Collections

The BC Archives holds a significant number of records relating to Indigenous people and communities. Many are provincial or colonial government records created by settlers about First Nations, but a number of records contain first-hand Indigenous accounts, including audio recordings of songs and ceremonies, photographs of communities and people, and transcripts of interviews with Indigenous people. At this time, the archives hold no records created by Indigenous communities or organizations, but a lot of significant information is held within records created by governments, as well as anthropologists and early Western settlers to the province. The information in archival records may be useful to support the process of repatriation.

I've built some really good relationships with museums. I love them! I love the people that work in them!

~ Willie White, Tsimshian Nation, weaver

We encourage online research using the databases above before you visit, to identify records you might be interested in. All visitors are required to register online for a BC Archives research pass: sales.royalbcmuseum.bc.ca/bcarchives

The following online archives resources may be helpful in your research:

BC Archives Collections Search

search-bcarchives.royalbcmuseum.bc.ca

Genealogy Search

search-collections.royalbcmuseum.bc.ca/Genealogy

Archives Library Search
voyager.library.uvic.ca:8000/vwebv/searchBasic?sk=en_US (bit.ly/UVicSearch)[5]

Visiting the BC Archives to conduct research and view original records is free; you can consult the Royal BC Museum website for opening hours. Since the archives collection consists of thousands of boxes, most of our records are held off site. Please call or email at least two days in advance of your visit so we can ensure the records you wish to look at are on site, ready for you:

BC Archives Reference Room
(250) 387-1952
access@royalbcmuseum.bc.ca

If you would like to arrange an orientation to the archives for your community, have a specific request about Indigenous materials held in the BC Archives, or would like to discuss the digital repatriation of archival materials in the BC Archives collection, you can contact our archivist who works with Indigenous communities and records:

Genevieve Weber, Archivist
(250) 886-4017
gweber@royalbcmuseum.bc.ca

If we are to truly advance reconciliation, we must undo the lasting damage that has resulted, and the Royal British Columbia Museum must play a role in this.
~ Jack Lohman CBE, CEO of the Royal BC Museum

5 For the convenience of those referencing the print version of this handbook, we have offered alternative, shortened URLs where appropriate.

PART 5

Repatriation from Other Institutions

Some countries or nation-states have laws that address repatriation for national museums or other government-funded museums and institutions. Most major museums, and some smaller ones, also have institutional policies on repatriation or deaccessioning human remains and tangible or intangible culture. There is a slow but steadily growing list of global museums that have begun addressing this work as well. Mainstream laws and policies can be helpful, but they can also be prohibitive, depending on the situation.

Indigenous Peoples have legal traditions and protocols that have guided Indigenous societies for thousands of years. When applied to repatriation, they have proven very effective in guiding Indigenous and museum people in diplomatic relations, negotiations and processes.

Repatriation is ultimately a human experience. How well a repatriation process goes can depend on factors such as the geographic and political climate and the cultures and personalities of the institutions and people involved. At the end of the day, relationships make the difference. Creating relationships built upon mutual respect, cooperation and trust has been key in building greater understanding of and respect for the Indigenous repatriation movement and is critical to finding and forging paths toward reconciliation.

The information below gives an overview of some of the different laws or approaches that some governments have created to address repatriation. To explore some global museums with repatriation or deaccessioning policies, see Appendix G: Global Museums with Major Indigenous Collections from BC.

When we work closely together with museums, the playing field is levelled. Museum policies and practices no longer override our beliefs and practices. Museums begin to understand us on our own terms, not just theirs.[6]

~ Jisgang Nika Collison, Executive Director,
Haida Gwaii Museum at K̲ay Llnagaay

The International Context

The United Nations (UN) is an international organization made up of almost 200 member states around the world. In 2007, after over two decades of work, the UN voted to adopt the UN Declaration on the Rights of Indigenous Peoples (UNDRIP) to preserve the rights that "constitute the minimum standards for the survival, dignity and well-being of the indigenous peoples of the world" (see Article 43) and that might not be protected under the laws or constitutions of nation-state governments.

Canada, the United States, Australia and New Zealand originally opposed UNDRIP, but have since signed on. Article 12 of UNDRIP directly addresses repatriation, but there are many sections in this declaration that can help support the work of repatriation. For more information visit:
un.org/development/desa/indigenouspeoples/declaration-on-the-rights-of-indigenous-peoples.html (bit.ly/UNDRIP2019)

6 See also: Nika Collison and Cara Krmpotich, "Saahlinda Naay—Saving Things House: The Haida Gwaii Museum Past, Present and Future" in *The Routledge Companion to Indigenous Repatriation: Return, Reconcile, Renew*, edited by Cressida Fforde, Honor Keeler and Tim McKeown (London, New York: Routledge, forthcoming).

indigenousfoundations.arts.ubc.ca/un_declaration_on_the_rights_of_indigenous_peoples (bit.ly/UBC-UNDRIP)

As well, check out this handy resource for learning about and planning for overseas repatriation:

A Guide to International Repatriation: Starting an Initiative in Your Community
Prepared by the Association on American Indian Affairs, USA.
indian-affairs.org/uploads/8/7/3/8/87380358/international_repatriation_guide.pdf (bit.ly/AGTIR)

> ***We as Indigenous people truly believe that the spirits of our Ancestors watch over us. Every ceremony that we conduct is proof of that.***
>
> ~ Honor Keeler, Cherokee Nation, Director, International Repatriation Project Association on American Indian Affairs

Canada

The Canadian government does not currently have legislation addressing the repatriation of Indigenous Ancestors and cultural heritage, but is working to create national support for repatriation through the legislation of Bill C-391, "An Act respecting a national strategy for the repatriation of Aboriginal cultural property." The act is still working its way through the system to achieve its final approval.

To stay current on the status of this Bill, visit: parl.ca/LegisInfo/BillDetails.aspx?billId=9614171 (bit.ly/C-391)

Some provinces have acts that address repatriation. The Province of BC does not yet have a repatriation act, but does have policy for its provincial museum. See Part 4: Repatriation from the Royal BC Museum to familiarize yourself with the Royal BC Museum and its approaches to repatriation.

The following provides an overview of some resources that exist that can be very helpful when pursuing repatriation in Canada.

Canadian Cultural Property Export Review Board

Canada has laws around the import and export of cultural property. While it was not created specifically for Indigenous repatriation, the Cultural Property Export and Import Act is good for private donors of treasures who would like a Cultural Properties tax receipt (which can sometimes be more beneficial than a regular tax receipt). Cultural Properties is also a venue to secure monies to assist in the purchase of objects of national significance that are being offered for sale. For more information, visit:

Nuu-chah-nulth baskets. Photo courtesy Lou-ann Neel.

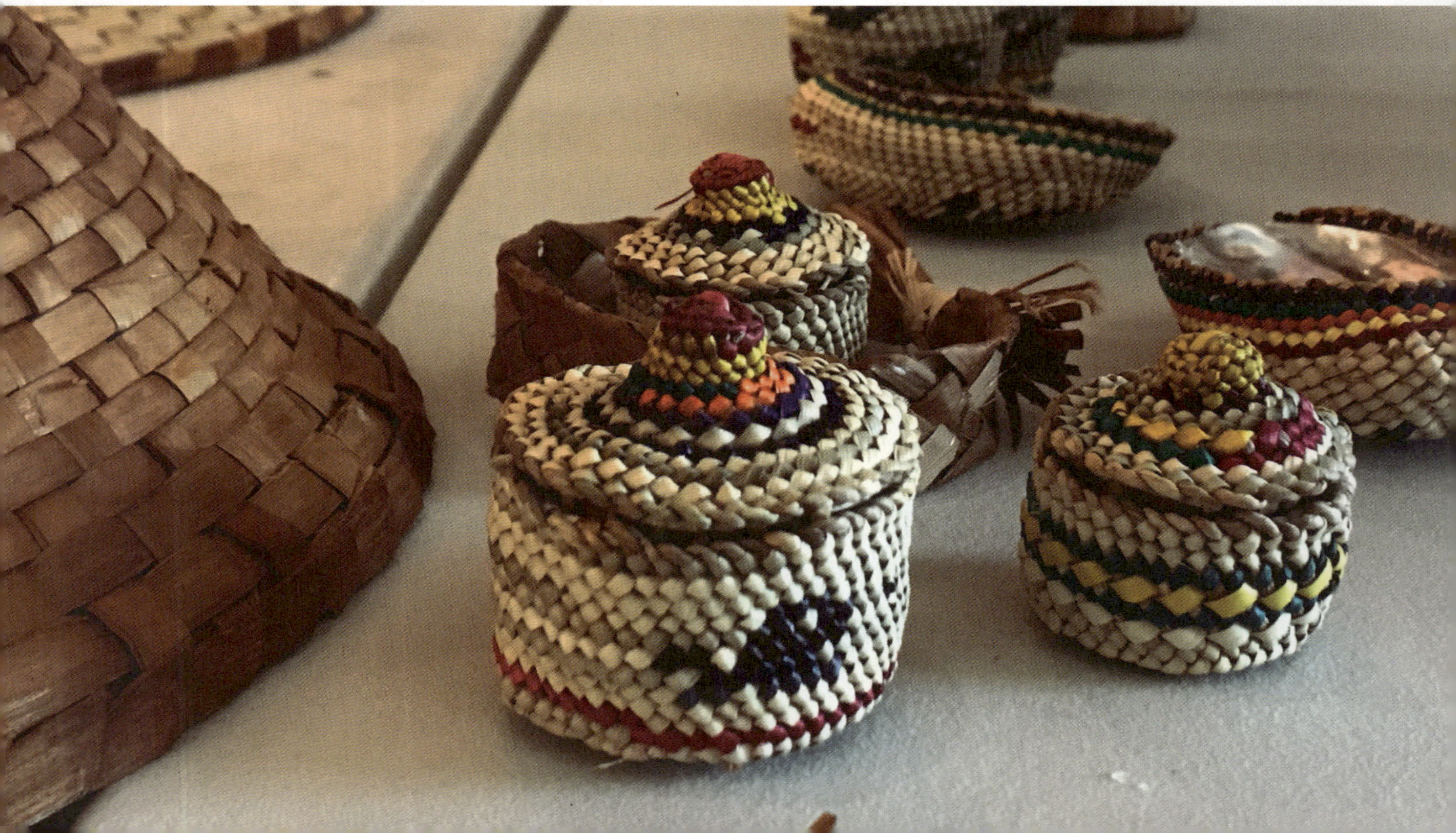

canada.ca/en/services/culture/history-heritage/movable-cultural-property/export-review-board.html (bit.ly/CCPexport)

Task Force Report on Museums and First Peoples

The Task Force Report on Museums and First Peoples (1994) is a very useful document created by the Assembly of First Nations and the Canadian Museums Association. The report's mission is "To develop ethical framework and strategies for Aboriginal Nations to represent their history and culture in concert with cultural institutions." While not legislation, it provides vision and guidance for the creation of healthy relationships between Indigenous Peoples and mainstream museums. To view the report, visit: museums.in1touch.org/uploaded/web/docs/Task_Force_Report_1994.pdf (bit.ly/TaskForce1994)

> ***What we know, and what so many of you know, is that outside the law and policy, the most effective repatriations that have occurred have done so because of diplomacy and relationship building.***
>
> ~ Jackie Swift, Repatriation Manager, Smithsonian National Museum of the American Indian, Comanche and Fort Sill Apache Tribes

Treaty Negotiations

Some Indigenous Nations are involved in treaty negotiations with Canada and the Province of BC. In these cases, the Canadian Museum of History and Royal BC Museum are bound to a repatriation treaty process, which is different than negotiating repatriations with non-government museums. Contact your Nation's treaty office to learn more.

Truth and Reconciliation Calls to Action: Museums and Archives

The TRC released their report in 2016 with 94 Calls to Action. Numbers 67 to 70 focus on relations between Indigenous Peoples and mainstream museums and archives. While repatriation is not specifically mentioned, adhering to UNDRIP and reconciliation are, both of which are directly related to repatriation. To view the Calls to Action, visit: nctr.ca/assets/reports/Calls_to_Action_English2.pdf (bit.ly/TRC-C2A)

Steering Committee on Canada's Archives: Response to the Report of the Truth and Reconciliation Commission Taskforce

The taskforce was formed in 2016 to respond to Truth and Reconciliation Commission (TRC) Call to Action Number 70, and it is working to develop ethical protocols and a reconciliation framework for archival institutions across Canada, which includes repatriation. To learn more, visit: archives2026.com/response-to-the-report-of-the-truth-and-reconciliation-commission-taskforce (bit.ly/TaskforceResponse)

We need to be able to look at the 94 TRC recommendations to say this applies to the work that we are doing here with the museum and with the government. Hand-in-hand collaboration.

~ Dan Smith, Nuyumbalees Cultural Centre, BC Museums Association Indigenous Advisory Chair

United States of America

In the United States, the Native American Graves Protection and Repatriation Act (NAGPRA) addresses repatriation as it relates to federally funded institutions, the exception being the Smithsonian Institute, which has its own repatriation act for both its National Museum of the American Indian and the National Museum of Natural History(see p. 131): americanindian.si.edu/sites/1/files/pdf/about/NMAIAct.pdf (bit.ly/NMAIact)

Institutions that are not federally funded are not bound by NAGPRA, but may still be active in repatriation.

Native American Graves Protection and Repatriation Act

In 1990, the United States government passed NAGPRA, which mandates that federally funded museums and agencies in the US repatriate Ancestral remains and certain cultural items back to federally recognized Native American tribes. Indigenous Nations living outside the US technically do not qualify to enter into the NAGPRA repatriation process, but this does not mean cross-border repatriation isn't possible. Don't forget there are two parties involved, and each brings their own ways to the table. Creativity, diplomacy and relationship-building are great at navigating bureaucracy. The Haida have brought home Haida Ancestors from four different institutions in the USA since 2002. To learn more about NAGPRA, visit: www.nps.gov/nagpra

National Museum of the American Indian Act

In 1989, the United States government passed the National Museum of the American Indian Act (NMAI Act). The law established the National Museum of the American Indian as part of the Smithsonian

Institution. The law also required the secretary of the Smithsonian to prepare an inventory of all American Indian and Native Hawaiian human remains and funerary objects in Smithsonian collections, as well as to return these items upon the request of culturally affiliated, federally recognized American Indian tribes and Native Hawaiian organizations.

The NMAI Act and NAGPRA are both human rights legislations for Native Peoples, and we shouldn't ever lose sight of that. In neither piece of legislation does it say there's any caveat for, on the back end, restrictions, conditions for repatriation. Once a repatriation has been conducted, nobody has the right to tell you what to do.

~ Jackie Swift, Repatriation Manager, Smithsonian NMAI, Comanche and Fort Sill Apache Tribes

United Kingdom

England's national museums, including the British Museum, the Natural History Museum and the National Museums Liverpool, are governed by the British Museum Act. The original act forbade repatriation or deaccessioning of collections, period. A few years ago, the act was amended to allow for the repatriation of human remains. At present, it is still "illegal" for England's national museums to repatriate objects, including burial goods. Other museums in England and Wales are not bound by the British Museum Act. For more on repatriation from England's national museums, visit:

Repatriation of Historic Human Remains: United Kingdom
loc.gov/law/help/repatriation-human-remains/united-kingdom.php (bit.ly/UKrepatriation)

British Museum Act
britishmuseum.org/PDF/BM1963Act.pdf

Amendment to the British Museum Act
publications.parliament.uk/pa/cm200910/cmbills/037/10037.i-i.html#j01 (bit.ly/BMA1963)

Museums in Scotland are governed by Scottish national law, which does not prohibit repatriation, in general. While not law, the Scottish National Development Body has developed guidelines for the care of human remains in their museums:

Guidelines for the Care of Human Remains in Scottish Museum Collections
museumsgalleriesscotland.org.uk/media/1089/guidelines-for-the-care-of-human-remains-in-scottish-museum-collections.pdf (bit.ly/ScottishRemains)

Museums Association—Scotland
museumsassociation.org/your-area/scotland

Germany

Germany does not have federal legislation addressing repatriation specifically, but some German states may have to seek approval from the government before a repatriation can occur. While not law, the German Museums Association has published ethical guidelines on the subject of repatriation and caring for collections:

German Museums Association: Recommendations for the Care of Human Remains in Museums and Collections
concernedhistorians.org/content_files/file/TO/296.pdf

German Museums Association: Guide on Dealing with Collections from Colonial Contexts
museumsbund.de/wp-content/uploads/2018/07/dmb-guidelines-colonial-context.pdf (bit.ly/ColonialCollections)

German Museums Association
museumsbund.de

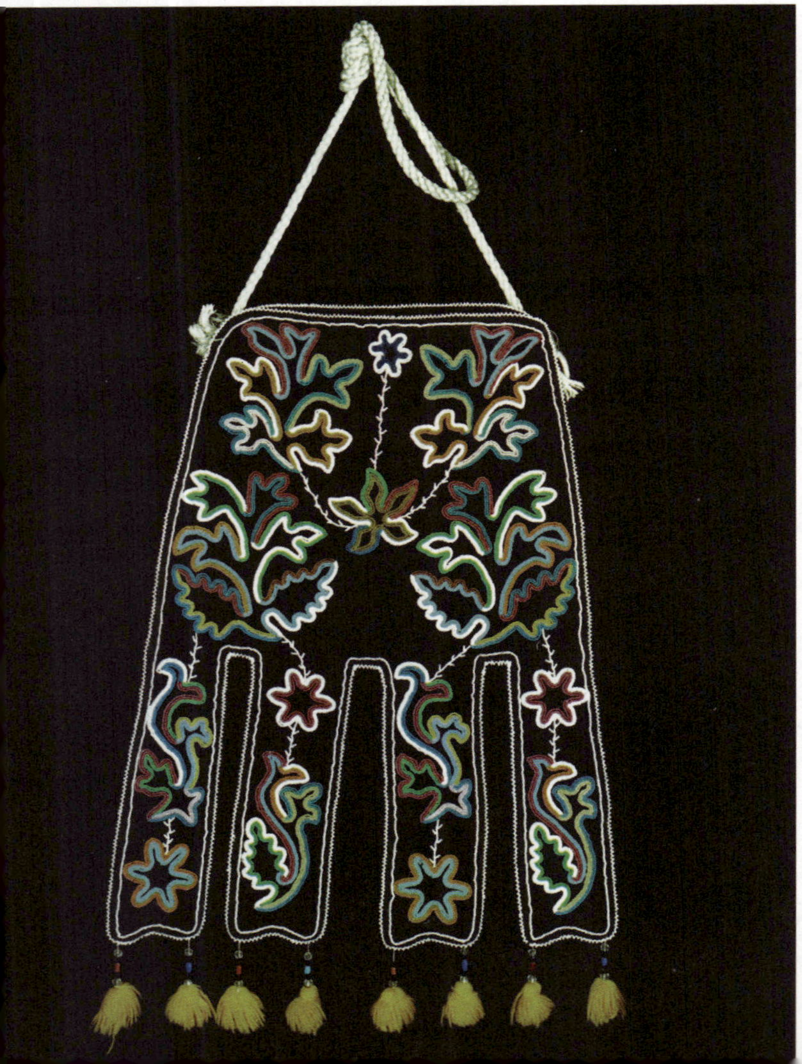

Octopus beaded bag, ethnology collection, RBCM146514.

Netherlands

The Netherlands does not have a federal law that addresses repatriation, but the Netherlands Museums Association has published guidelines for the deaccessioning of objects in Dutch museums: Leidraad Afstoten Museale Objecten, also known as the Guideline for Deaccessioning Museum Objects, which includes an excerpt from the International Council of Museums' Code of Ethics for Museums noting that museums are to develop their own deaccessioning policies, including deaccessioning objects for the purpose of repatriation. In 2016, the Cultural Heritage Agency of the Netherlands created the Heritage Act, which includes provisions on the international return of cultural property. The Netherlands Museums Association also manages a Deaccessions Database, where museums can present public information regarding museum objects they plan to deaccession:

Netherlands Museums Association Guideline for Deaccessioning Museum Objects
museumvereniging.nl/media/lamo_2016_guidelines_for_the_deaccessioning_of_museum_objects_1.pdf (bit.ly/NMAguideline)

Cultural Heritage Agency of the Netherlands Heritage Act
cultureelerfgoed.nl/sites/default/files/publications/heritage-act-2016.pdf (bit.ly/CHANheritage)

Netherlands Museums Association Deaccessions Database
afstotingsdatabase.nl

Netherlands Museums Association
museumvereniging.nl/english

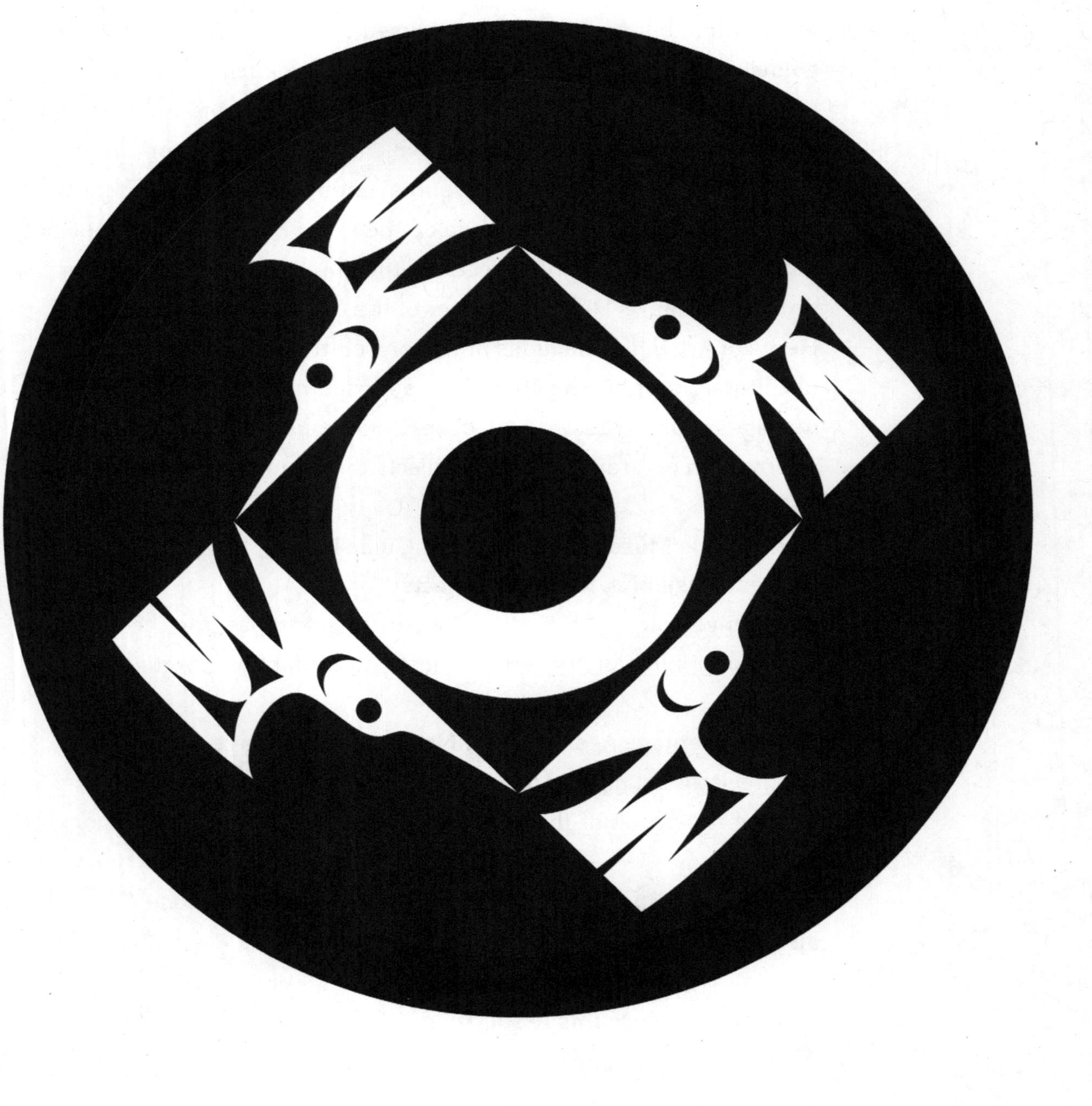

PART 6

For Institutions Wishing to Repatriate to Indigenous Peoples in BC

Once the Royal BC Museum started talking about the goal of creating an Indigenous repatriation handbook, colleagues from other museums started asking us for advice on how to repatriate to Indigenous communities in BC. This added another layer to the handbook, and we hope to be able to assist in connecting museums to Indigenous Nations in BC. First of all, we would like to acknowledge how amazing it is that you are at a place where repatriation is a priority!

We are in a new era where the TRC, UNDRIP, Task Force Report on Museums and First Peoples, and NAGPRA and the NMAI Act are strongly encouraging or requiring museums, archives and universities with Indigenous belongings to do things in a more respectful way. Repatriation can be so rewarding for institutions, and although it is time-consuming and absorbs many human and financial resources, the benefits are far-reaching and go beyond doing the right thing.

Learning and Reaching Out

One of the first steps in repatriating to Indigenous Peoples in British Columbia is to know more about us. Reaching out to the Indigenous Nations, looking at their official websites and reading their recommended resources are good steps. If you need advice

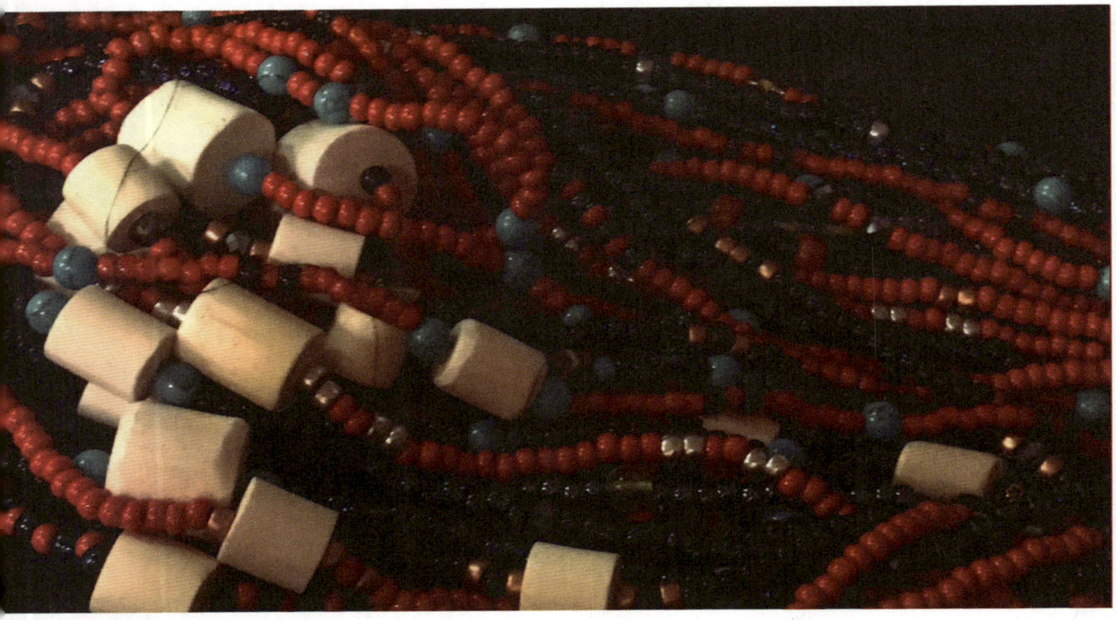

Devil's club necklaces worn as protection by many coastal First Nations when preparing Ancestral remains.

on how to reach out to these Nations and communities, please do not hesitate to ask Lou-ann Neel at lneel@royalbcmuseum.bc.ca.

You can also use the handbook available from the Union of BC Indian Chiefs: ubcic.bc.ca

or the Guide to Indigenous Organizations and Services in BC produced by the Ministry of Indigenous Relations and Reconciliation to help identify the Nations of BC: www2.gov.bc.ca/gov/content/governments/indigenous-people/aboriginal-organizations-services (bit.ly/IOS-BC)

This webpage includes one of the most comprehensive listings of First Nations and Indigenous organizations in BC. The list can be downloaded as an Excel spreadsheet and sorted as required.

You can also find out about archaeological projects within a given community or territory by contacting the BC Archaeology Branch and providing them with a map of the area you're interested in. They can be reached at (250) 953-3334, or at this link: archdatarequest.nrs.gov.bc.ca

It is important to establish a respectful relationship with the Indigenous Peoples you are repatriating to. Community visits are important and bring long-term benefits to your museum. Museum employees who immerse themselves in Indigenous communities, make Indigenous friends and meet Indigenous colleagues, and participate in Indigenous events have proven to bring the museum further in its reconciliation journey.

> ***We all belong together, and we all learn from each other. It doesn't matter what race or Nation you are from. Once we start cooperating, this whole world will get a lot better and stronger, and it'll be easier for our children to fight for what we believe in.***
>
> ~Vern Williams Jr., Haida song composer,
> Haida Repatriation Committee

Getting Organized

Being organized and having clear policies is key to successful repatriation.

Policy and Procedures

It is important to update policies and procedures regarding Indigenous collections and repatriation on a regular basis. As we move into a reconciliation era, museums have the responsibility to reconcile for the thousands of Indigenous cultural objects and Ancestral remains in their care. The Royal BC Museum's policy had not been updated in 20 years. In 2018, the policy was updated to better reflect the museum's response to the TRC and our strong commitment to the repatriation of tangible and intangible heritage. Procedures were also updated to ensure repatriation could be done with the least amount of bureaucracy, especially for Ancestral remains.

Records Management

Being prepared for repatriation is important, and it can take a lot of resources to be repatriation-ready. It is important to compile all of the associated records with the cultural object or Ancestral remains being repatriated. Having these records available to the Indigenous Nations early on is important for their research. Updating the museum records with Indigenous Peoples' feedback is also necessary.

At the Royal BC Museum, we have new staff and students to help connect the records with the Ancestral remains and the audio-visual collections, knowing that these are priorities for Indigenous communities to repatriate.

Being Ready to Repatriate Ancestral Remains

With the added sensitivities around Ancestral remains repatriation, it is important to care for Ancestral remains and associated burial items with the utmost respect while they are in the care of museums. For those of you who care for Ancestral remains and burial items, it is important to ask yourself if there is anything else you can do to respectfully care for them while they are in your care.

Lucy Bell, the head of the Indigenous Collections and Repatriation Department at the Royal BC Museum, asked this of herself and her team when she began working at the museum. She also asked if we were ready to do quick returns of Ancestral remains if an Indigenous community told us they wanted the remains returned immediately. The team went to work connecting Ancestral remains with their associated documents. This was a six-month process that often involved connecting with the BC Archaeology Branch, the RCMP, the coroner's office and descendants of collectors to find out all we could about the Ancestral remains in the museum. In some cases, this research continues.

The next step was to be more respectful of the Ancestral remains. It is important for museums to remember that these are human beings, and we should treat them as deceased loved ones as best as we can. For Lucy, that meant re-examining how they were stored. The team spent a week taking Ancestral remains out of the plastic bags and re-wrapping them in cotton fabric. The Ancestral remains were then sorted by Nation, and a small ceremony was held with local Elders. This was a quiet, private event at the museum, but all staff were made aware of the important work being done.

Creating ceremonial space is also a consideration. Providing a place for smudging, food-burning, feasting, singing and dancing is a must. In tight museum spaces, it is important to think outside the box. Maybe the ceremonial space is in the museum's classroom or staffroom, or even in the neighbouring Indigenous Nation's community. This is a highly personal decision for the Indigenous visitors.

A quick checklist can help the museum prepare for Ancestral remains repatriation to go smoothly. This is the Royal BC Museum's basic checklist:

Jaalen and Gwaai Edenshaw doing research for the film *Edge of the Knife*.

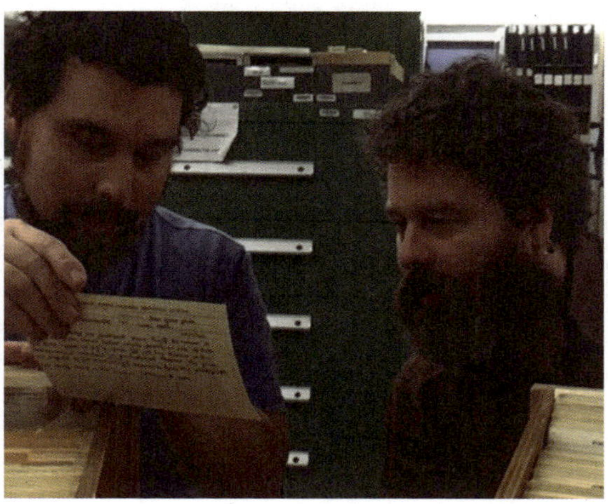

Table 2.
RBCM repatriation planning checklist.

STEP	DETAILS
Network with Indigenous repatriation representatives	Determine the forthcoming repatriation request
Plan the repatriation event at the museum	Discuss timeline, expectations and process with communities and staff
Receive formal request	Give heads-up to executive, collections committee and staff with Indigenous Collections and Repatriation Department's recommendations
Continue discussions between requesting community and the museum	Ask for community guidance re: • size of delegation • number of Elders (to ensure seating) • accessibility requirements • timeline • agenda for repatriation day • care and handling • storage/shipping • space requirements • ceremonial requirements • parking requirements • visit to other collections • involvement of museum staff
Identify any burial objects; assess request for overlap with other First Nation groups	Create a supporting document package to be given to communities along with Ancestral remains; seek guidance from the Indigenous Advocacy and Advisory Council if necessary
Prepare repatriation paperwork	Museum CEO and community representative sign documents confirming museum's intention to repatriate material in advance of return
Prepare Ancestral remains	Ensure museum departments know of the repatriation ceremony taking place on site • Delegate tasks • Determine expenses • Have paperwork
Return Ancestral remains and associated documents and material	Guided by community, particularly with respect to any protocols and related ceremonies that need to take place; community representative taking custody of Ancestral remains signs documents
Submit repatriation paperwork to the Indigenous Advocacy and Advisory Council and registrar to notify collections committee/board	Ensure information is included in any required museum reports
Debrief	Debrief session with staff; follow-up call with repatriation committee representatives

PART 7

Case Study: Repatriation Journey of the Haida Nation[7]

> ***My mother said you have to be so careful, because your actions will have bearing on your children and your grandchildren, and everybody to come after. So how you conduct yourself is very important. My first lesson on anything was respect for all things.[8]***
>
> ~ GwaaG̲anad Diane Brown

One of the main laws of the Haida Nation is Yahguudangang (respect), meaning respect for all things: land, water and air; the Supernatural; our Ancestors and each other. It is only when we show such respect that we can be worthy of respect ourselves. From this law, and many others of our Nation, comes the privilege of responsibility.

7 See also: Nika Collison and Cara Krmpotich, "Saahlinda Naay—Saving Things House: The Haida Gwaii Museum Past, Present and Future" in *The Routledge Companion to Indigenous Repatriation: Return, Reconcile, Renew*, edited by Cressida Fforde, Honor Keeler and Tim McKeown (London, New York: Routledge, forthcoming).

8 GwaaG̲anad, Diane Brown in *Gina Suuda Tl'l X̲asii ~ Came to Tell Something: Art & Artist in Haida Society*, edited by Nika Collison (Skidegate, Haida Gwaii: Haida Gwaii Museum Press, 2014), 111.

As museum professionals and as human beings, we carry the responsibility to effect societal change by mainstreaming Canada's dark history with Indigenous Peoples while actively working to set things right. In the Haida–mainstream museum world, the path toward reconciliation has been shaped by Yahguudangang: the act of paying respect. The Haida Nation sees this work, which includes repatriation, as based upon mutual respect, cooperation and trust.[9]

Our Ancestors, cultural treasures and intangible heritage mean more to the Haida Nation than anything else in the world. All are integral links to our past, are critical to our present-day life, and provide guidance and a way forward for our future. Yahguudangang not only helps us heal, learn and become empowered, it also helps us better understand and address the history of Indigenous Peoples and Canada.

The repatriation of Haida Ancestors first occurred through a stand taken to stop the ongoing practice of colonial collecting, by pursuing the collectors themselves. In the 1980s, two separate Canadian archaeologists conducted unethical digs on Haida Gwaii. The Skidegate Band Council, Old Massett Village Council and RCMP worked with the then-new director of the Haida Gwaii Museum, Nathalie Macfarlane, to retrieve our Ancestors and cultural treasures, which were returned in the early 1990s.

The repatriation of Haida Ancestors from museums and universities began with the Haida Repatriation Committee, a volunteer working group formed in the mid-1990s through the vision of Lucy Bell. Lucy was then an intern at the Royal BC Museum. When working late one night, she heard children running and playing in the museum stairwell, but there were no children in the building—the museum was closed. Lucy learned there were Indigenous Ancestral remains held in the museum, and that other museums held them as well.

9 Jennifer Shannon, Sonya Atalay, Jisgang Nika Collison, Te Herekiekie Herewini, Eric Hollinger, Michelle Horwood, Robert W. Preucel, Anthony Shelton and Paul Tapsell, "Ritual Processes of Repatriation: A Discussion," *Museum Worlds* 5 (1): 89–90, doi.org/10.3167/armw.2017.050109

She realized she had heard the spirits of children, and that she'd been called to bring home the remains of her people. When Lucy moved home, she was hired by the Old Massett Village Council Heritage Resources and got to work, rallying the community. In 1998, the first repatriation of Haida Ancestors from a mainstream museum was successfully negotiated with the Royal BC Museum.

For many years, the Haida Gwaii Museum and Haida Heritage and Repatriation Society sent letters to museums around the world, requesting inventories of Haida collections and asking if these institutions also held Haida Ancestral remains. Over 130 institutions have been contacted, and there are still many more to seek out. Ten of the institutions held Ancestral remains from Haida Gwaii.

From the inventories compiled, we know of over 12,000 objects attributed as "Haida" that are held in museums around the world. The majority of pieces in these collections are cultural belongings; some are works made for the commercial market, both historically and in modern times; and some of the attributions assigned to some pieces need to be revisited. Also, many collections are identified only as "Northwest Coast," and, just as some objects have been incorrectly attributed as "Haida," so have some Haida treasures been misattributed to other Nations. There is still a lot of work to be done regarding attributions and correcting museum records in general.

As this information came in from museums, it was presented to the Haida Repatriation Committee and then to the greater Haida Nation. Many consultation and planning meetings were held. The direction received was to focus on bringing our Ancestors home and to build positive relationships with museums along the way, then to bring home more of our family heirlooms and cultural heritage.

To date, over 500 of our relatives have been brought home from across North America, and one from the UK. This number includes four voluntary repatriations from individuals who contacted the Haida when they learned through the media about our work in repatriation and realized they should not have what they did. The project has easily cost over $1,000,000 in raised funds, in-kind donations and sweat-labour to find our Ancestors and bring them home with honour and respect. We are currently in the middle of preparing to bring home and re-inter the last of our Ancestors taken from Haida Gwaii (that we are aware of).

Retrieving our relatives' bones from museums is not "traditional," yet it has become part of our way of life. Yahguudangang cannot be achieved by the Haida Repatriation Committee, Haida Gwaii Museum and Haida Heritage and Repatriation Society alone. It requires the commitment of our Nation, from the youngest child to the eldest of Elders, and the support of our growing allies in the world.

Our children travel to museums with us to bring their Ancestors home. They help to carry these Ancestors, wrapped in button blankets the children have sewn, contained in the handmade bentwood boxes they have helped paint, to the graveyard for final burial. Ceremonial leaders and Elders guide, teach and protect us. The community fundraises to support Yahguudangang initiatives and prepares for reburials and community feasts. We travel in large groups, bringing youth, Hereditary Leaders, Matriarchs, artists, Elders, fluent speakers, ceremonial leaders, scholars and others to museums, and we reach out to our Haida relatives living nearby.

When we travel to museums, we visit our treasures and other containers of knowledge, such as archives. From utilitarian to ceremonial, these works demonstrate the refined understanding that our Ancestors had of art and architecture, engineering and science, sociology and philosophy, and medicine, and of co-existing with the Supernatural, Haida Gwaii and each other. No, we were not perfect, but there is wisdom in that historical knowledge that we apply today to help address and solve modern problems and needs, and our Elders guide us in this.

We bring our cultural diaspora home through imagery, audio recordings, collection notes and the re-creation of Ancestral cultural treasures—and through the physical, emotional and spiritual connections that forever bind us. A few times, treasures have come home from these museums. We are now ready to bring home much more. But we don't have another 20 years, or another million-plus dollars. We need more response, more commitment—more decolonization from mainstream museums and from nation-state governments.

Yahguudangang honours and pays respect to our Ancestors and heritage, but doing the work can be difficult. It can bring out emotions that are confusing and not linear: anger, excitement, grief, joy, horror, laughter, awe and sometimes, nothing at all. Emotional numbing. But because of the work we are doing, we can address this heartache and use it to make good in our Nation and in the world.

When we work closely together with museums, the playing field is levelled. Museum policies and practices no longer override Haida beliefs and practices, and museum staff begin to understand us on Haida terms, not just their terms. Approaching Yahguudangang with the goal of mutual respect, cooperation and trust has led to some museums joining us in *wanting* to see our Ancestors and heritage come home rather than these institutions *having* to repatriate them back to us. Yahguudangang has also resulted in some valued, ongoing relationships with museums and their staff.

We strive to have the work achieved through Yahguudangang celebrated in all forms: news media, publications, documentaries, and conferences and lectures. This continues to open the eyes not only of institutions, but of the public, who have rapidly come to support the work our Nation and mainstream museums are doing together. Being exposed to Yahguudangang also inspires our own people to become more and more involved in finding a variety of paths toward reconciliation.

Many Haida have gone on to secure museum internships or careers in Indigenous language, arts and heritage once becoming involved in Yahguudangang, shifting social discourse for the better in the process. Many collaborative exhibitions, publications, programs, etc. have occurred because of Yahguudangang. As well, Haida Nation–based scholarship is valued on the same level as Western academia, and is now regarded as critical to progressive museum work. In this, our history is shared in a sensible arrangement with the museums, and artists and other Haida scholars have much easier access to learn from their heritage.

The healing of Yahguudangang is felt deeply. While it cannot be measured, it is visible in the way we live our lives: the way we talk and interact, and the choices we make. As demonstrated above, the healing is not only ours. Yahguudangang provides opportunity for Western museums to become voluntary agents of change, rather than the physical evidence of Canada's genocide against Indigenous Peoples. When museums support our repatriation efforts, it helps museum staff address or heal from the shame of colonialism many carry. The bigger shame, then, becomes not working toward repatriation.

Working with mainstream museums to repair some of our shared history has brought two worlds together, and is in fact creating a new world. Yahguudangang is not quick, easy or pretty; it is complicated, powerful and transformative. Yahguudangang is a way of life: a dedication to our Ancestors, to tl'l yahda (making things right), and to our future generations.

Haida Repatriation Organizational Structure

The Haida Gwaii Museum and the Haida Heritage and Repatriation Society (previously Old Massett Heritage Resources) facilitate the work of repatriation. Two volunteer committees, the Skidegate Repatriation and Cultural Committee and the Old Massett Repatriation and Cultural Committee, work with their respective communities to provide information on repatriation, receive guidance, fundraise and organize. Together, these committees operate as the Haida Repatriation Committee, working with the Haida Gwaii Museum and the Haida Heritage and Repatriation Society to build relationships with mainstream museums, bring our Ancestors home, breathe life into our treasures, and continue to move the work of Yahg̲uudangang forward.

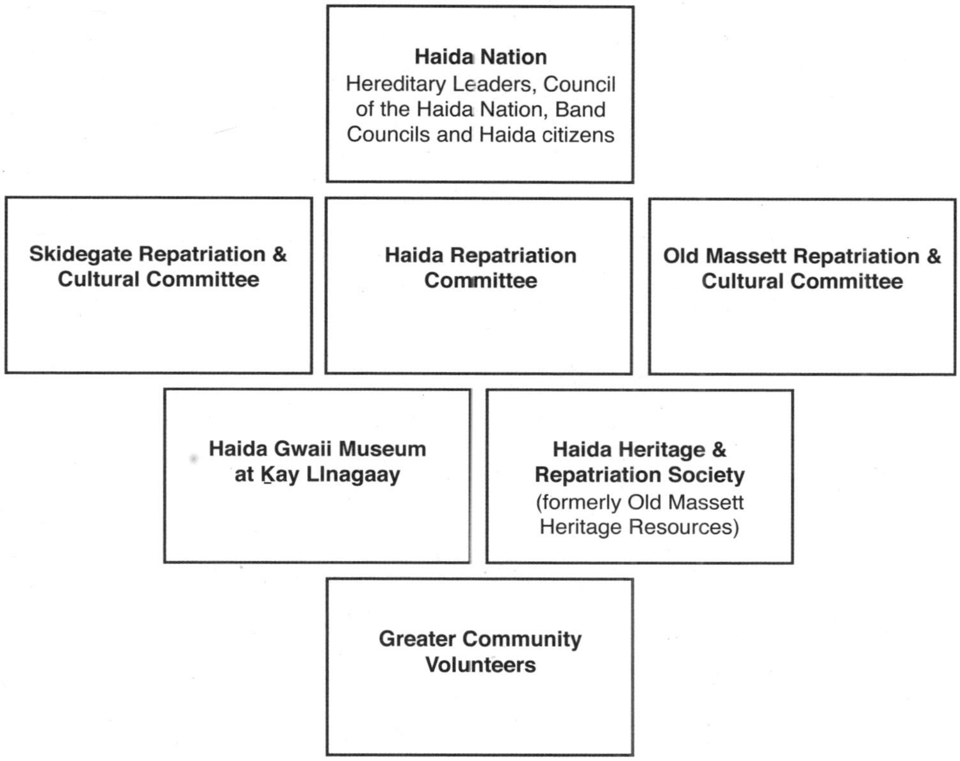

Haida Nation community committee organizational structure. Image courtesy Haida Gwaii Museum at K̲ay Llnagaay.

APPENDIX A

Glossary of Terms

Accession: The acquisition of objects into a museum collection. Once it is added to the collection, it is given an accession number.

Ancestral remains: Human skeletal remains that have an Ancestral connection to Indigenous Peoples of today.

Anthropology: The study of humans and human behaviour.

Archaeology: The scientific study of human history through the study of sites, burials and human-worked materials (i.e., belongings or artifacts) generally acquired through archaeological excavations or found by chance.

Archaeological objects and materials: Any material or information that tells us about human activity in the past. This includes artifacts or belongings as well as non-artifactual materials; e.g., soil, middens, animal bones, food remains, samples, field notes, photos, maps and any associated data recovered from an archaeological site.

Archives: This term can refer to archival records (primary source historical records), the institution responsible for the care and control of archival records, or the repository in which archival records are stored and preserved.

Artifact: Any object made or modified for use by humans.

Associated burial objects: Objects that, by their attributes or location, can be demonstrated to have been placed in direct association with the burial of a human being as part of the burial rite.

Associated records: Records illustrating and illuminating the story of the acquisition of Indigenous collections, including collectors' notes, catalogue records, photographs, audio-visual records, research notes and reports.

Belongings: Cultural objects, intangible cultural heritage, material culture, intellectual properties, etc., that are of Indigenous origin.

Contemporary work of art: Representation made in any medium by an artist or artists of Indigenous origin, particularly, but not exclusively, since 1951 after the Potlatch Ban was lifted.

Cultural objects: Anything created by humans that gives information about the culture of its creator and users. This often refers to portable items such as tools, canoes, poles, etc., and is differentiated from features on the landscape that were made by humans and also give information about the culture of its creators—these are referred to as *cultural sites*.

Custodial agreement: An agreement between a museum and an Indigenous government providing for the sharing of management, interpretation, display and possession of objects in a museum collection.

Deaccession: To remove an object from a museum collection.

Ethnography: The branch of anthropology that deals with the scientific description of specific human societies.

Ethnographic objects: Objects, other than archaeological artifacts, originating with and/or used by Indigenous people and representative of their culture at a particular period.

Ethnology: A branch of anthropology that analyzes and compares different peoples, especially in regard to their historical development.

Human remains: Skeletal remains not necessarily identified as Indigenous.

Indigenous: The original peoples of Canada, including people of First Nations, Inuit and Métis ancestry.

Intangible cultural heritage: The practices, representations and expressions, as well as the knowledge and skills that communities, groups and, in some cases, individuals recognize as part of their cultural heritage.

Intellectual property: The rights one has to songs, oral histories, names, crests and other intangible cultural heritage.

Material culture: The physical aspect of culture in the objects that surround people. It includes usage, consumption, creation and trade of objects as well as the behaviours, norms and rituals that the objects create or take part in.

Midden: An ancient dumping ground for domestic waste, which may consist of animal bone, botanical materials, shells, lithics and artifacts.

Museology: The science or profession of museum organization and management.

Repatriation: The return to the country of origin. For museums, repatriation applies more specifically to the return of human remains and cultural objects to Indigenous communities.

Tangible cultural heritage: Includes buildings and historic places, monuments, artifacts, etc., which are considered worthy of preservation for the future. These include objects significant to the archaeology, architecture, science or technology of a specific culture.

Treaty: The constitutional and moral basis of alliance between Indigenous Peoples and Canada. Many Indigenous governments in Canada are in treaty negotiations, which include the repatriation of cultural objects from the Royal BC Museum and the Canadian Museum of History.

APPENDIX B

Indigenous Museums and Cultural Centres in Canada

This list is not comprehensive.

British Columbia

- Canoe Creek Cultural Program
- Coqualeetza Cultural Education Centre
- Cowichan Tribes Cultural Program
- Haida Gwaii Museum at Kay Llnagaay
- Haida Heritage Centre at Kay Llnagaay
- Heiltsuk Cultural Education Centre
- 'Ksan Historical Village
- Lake Babine Cultural Program
- Mount Currie Cultural Program
- Musqueam Cultural Education Resource Centre
- 'Namgis Cultural Program
- Nisga'a Museum
- Nuxalk Cultural Centre
- Nuyumbalees Cultural Centre
- En'owkin Cultural Centre
- Saanich Native Heritage Society
- Secwepemc Cultural Education Society
- Squamish-Lil'wat Cultural Centre
- Stó:lō Nation Cultural Program
- Stoney Creek Elders Cultural Society

- Tla'amin Cultural Centre
- U'mista Cultural Centre

Alberta

- Beaver Lake Cultural Program
- Frog Lake Cultural Program
- Kehewin Community Education Centre
- Maskwacis Cultural College
- Ninastako Cultural Centre
- Oldman River Cultural Centre
- Saddle Lake Cultural Education Program
- Siksika Cultural Centre
- Sarcee Culture Program
- Stoney Nation Education Authority

Saskatchewan

- Saskatchewan Indigenous Cultural Centre

Manitoba

- Brokenhead Cultural Program
- Cross Lake Band
- Dakota Ojibway Tribal Council
- Interlake Reserves Tribal Council Inc.
- Manitoba Indigenous Cultural Education Centre Inc.
- Norway House Cree Nation—Education, Training and Culture Division
- Peguis Cultural Centre
- Rolling River Cultural Education Program
- Sagkeeng Heritage Centre

- Tootinaowaziibeeng Community Cultural Centre
- West Region Tribal Council

Ontario

- Batchewana First Nation
- Lake of the Woods Ojibway Cultural Centre
- Native North American Travelling College
- Ojibway and Cree Cultural Centre
- Ojibwe Cultural Foundation
- Oneida Language and Cultural Centre
- Wikwemikong Interpretive/Heritage Centre
- Woodland Cultural Centre

Quebec

- Centre culturel Amikwan
- Centre culturel de Wanaskoademek
- Conseil de la Nation Atikamekw
- Conseil de la Nation huronne-wendat
- Conseil des Montagnais du Lac St-Jean
- Institut culturel et éducatif montagnais
- Aanischaaukamikw, the Cree Cultural Institute
- Kanehsatà:ke Education Center
- Kanien'kehá:ka Onkwawén:na Raotitióhkwa Language and Cultural Center
- Kitigan Zibi Education Council
- Listuguj Arts and Cultural Center
- Micmacs of Gesgapegiag

APPENDIX C

Organizational Templates, Procedures and Examples

The following documents can help you with logistical planning. For more great tips and templates, check out this online toolbox: artscapediy.org/Creative-Placemaking-Toolbox/How-Do-I-Use-This-Toolbox.aspx (bit.ly/PlacemakingToolbox)

Repatriation Committee Planning Template

Philosophies and Beliefs

What are our individual and collective philosophies and beliefs about the work we wish to do together as a committee, group or organization? How can we express our philosophies and beliefs in a way that will help to guide our work as committees, groups or organizations?

For example: Our people have been here in these lands we call (the word or phrases in your language that describes the lands/waterways/territories) since time immemorial; we believe in and practise all our social, political, economic, cultural and legal ways in the manner our people have always practised and recognized. These foundational philosophies and beliefs help to shape our current practices and guide our work to create policies and processes that support us as we maintain these practices for the benefit of our people and for generations to come.

Principles

What are the principles upon which our community builds our committees, groups or organizations? How can we express our principles in a way that will help guide our work as committees, groups or organizations?

For example: Our principles and the way we conduct ourselves maintain strong levels of respect, integrity, honour, trust, accountability, responsibility and mindfulness.

Values

What do we value as members of our community? How can we express our values in a way that will help guide our work as committees, groups or organizations?

For example: We value safety, wellness, and supportive spaces for all people of all ages in our communities. We value the right of all our people to be consulted and to be involved in all levels of community building, and therefore to develop systems and processes that demonstrate our commitment to openness, accountability and transparency.

Vision

What do we envision for our community through the work we will carry out as a committee, group or organization? How can we express our vision in a way that will help guide our work as committees, groups or organizations?

For example: We envision a day when our Ancestors' remains are returned to their resting places, and our cultural belongings have been returned to our people. We envision a day when all our people can gather to celebrate our accomplishments in the practice of our cultural ways.

Mission

A mission statement is usually one sentence. It is clear and concise.

For example: Our mission is to develop plans, strategies and actions that will result in the Ancestral remains and cultural belongings of our people being returned to their respective home communities.

Mandate

A mandate statement clarifies how your committee, group or organization will achieve its mission and realize its vision.

For example: Our mandate is:

1. To locate, identify and convey requests for the return of our Ancestors' remains and other cultural belongings from museums, post-secondary institutions, galleries and any other public and private entities currently housing the remains of our Ancestors.
2. To apply for funding and fundraise as needed to cover the costs associated with the repatriation of our Ancestors' remains and cultural belongings.

Strategies

A strategy is a higher-level statement about the broad approach or method that will guide the activities and actions that help you to meet your mandate, achieve your mission and ultimately realize your vision. Strategies can be thought of in several ways.

Funding Strategies

Funding strategies may include various types of annual grant funding, specific project funding, funding through a First Nation, treaty-related funding, and research funding.

Communication Strategies

Communication strategies may focus on strategies for updating the community, communicating with appropriate museum contacts and government officials, and media coverage.

Travel and Transportation Strategies

Travel and transportation strategies may include seeking special rates through local, national, and international air and ground travel and shipping services.

Goals and Objectives

Setting goals and clarifying the objectives is an important step that can enable the committee, group or organization to move ahead successfully. One way to create realistic goals is to include an initial timeline for each goal.

Table 3. Setting basic goals and timelines.

COMMITTEE GOAL AND OBJECTIVE STATEMENTS	TIMELINE
Goal 1: Request and complete the return of our Ancestors' remains from the RBCM	by December 31, 2019
Objective 1: To begin the process of repatriating Ancestral remains from museums in BC	
Goal 2: Request and complete the return of cultural belongings from the RBCM	by December 31, 2020
Objective 2: To begin the process of repatriation of cultural belongings from museums in BC	

Actions

Actions are practical, measurable activities that can be used to expand upon the initial timeline of the project's work plan.

Table 4. Action planning.

ACTION	TIMELINE	PERSON RESPONSIBLE	OUTCOME/DELIVERABLE
Prepare contact list and mailing labels for letters to museums	by May 1	Administrative support	Contact list that can be accessed and updated as required Mailing labels ready for letters
Draft letter to museums requesting repatriation of specific items	by May 10	Repatriation project coordinator	Draft letter for review, approval and signature of repatriation committee
Send repatriation letters to museums	by May 31	Repatriation project coordinator, administrative support and repatriation committee	Signed letters printed, copies made for project files, labels on envelopes, letters mailed, follow-up date established with committee

Sample Terms of Reference

Introduction

Over the past 50 years, our people have identified numerous Canadian museums and public post-secondary institutions that house the remains of our Ancestors and other important cultural belongings from our Nation. We believe that other museums and post-secondary institutions in other countries also house remains of our Ancestors and cultural belongings, and we believe it is important to begin the process of locating them and arranging for their return.

The return of our belongings will serve as an important step in our individual, familial and collective healing, and help us to rebuild that which was lost or fallen out of practice as a result of the removal of tangible and intangible cultural belongings of our Nation.

Background

In the past three years, through various short-term funding opportunities, our Nation has hired student researchers who have contacted museums across Canada to identify those that house the remains of our Ancestors. While carrying out this research, students also found cultural belongings ranging from everyday, utilitarian objects to items used only in ceremony.

Many of these belongings were taken out of our communities during the period of the Indian Act's Potlatch Ban (1867–1951) or during times of duress, which would have included the 10 years immediately following the removal of the Potlatch Ban from the Indian Act.

Our Nation's Youth Group and our Elders' Committee have both recommended that Council establish a Repatriation Committee that would review the research that has been conducted and develop a course of action to ensure the return of our belongings.

On (*date*), Council passed a motion to establish a Repatriation Committee (*see attached, enclose a copy of the Band Council Resolution*). A draft Terms of Reference for the Repatriation Committee has been created by Council, and will be finalized once the Repatriation Committee is established and has an opportunity to discuss it and make any edits.

Purpose

The purpose of the Repatriation Committee is to ensure the safe return of Ancestral remains and cultural belongings from our Nation.

Structure

The Repatriation Committee is a Special Project Committee established by Council, and as such, will have ongoing organizational and administrative support through the Council's office.

Members

According to our traditional decision-making structures and systems, members of the Repatriation Committee are (*describe who members are, who they represent, and how they are appointed*).

Roles and Responsibilities

Committee members will appoint a chairperson whose primary role is to serve as a moderator for meetings, and who is responsible for ensuring a record of meetings and decisions are created and shared with Council (i.e., meeting notes/summary of discussions and decisions).

The chairperson will ensure all members have an opportunity to provide input to committee discussions. As noted, Council's administrative staff will support this work.

The role of members will be to actively participate in all committee meetings to ensure their respective family groups have a voice in all aspects of the committee's work. Overall, the role and responsibility of the committee is to discuss, plan and recommend courses of action to be undertaken by Council in support of the Nation's work around repatriation.

Meetings

A meeting schedule will be developed at the committee's first meeting.

Decision-Making Processes

Decision-making processes will be discussed and determined at the committee's first meeting.

Scope of Authority

Since members of the Repatriation Committee represent each family group of our Nation, the committee's scope of authority will involve:

- The authority to set priorities and processes relating to repatriation, ensuring that the intent and outcome of these decisions benefits our Nation as a whole.

- The authority to make recommendations to Council regarding policies, processes, actions and fiscal decisions related to the process of repatriation.

Any administrative or operational steps or actions requiring funding approval will remain with Council, as funding agreements are part of Council's authority and responsibility.

Reporting Requirements

As a Special Project Committee of Council, the Repatriation Committee will provide quarterly reports to Council detailing the work of the committee for that reporting period. Reports will include a summary of committee meeting notes or minutes with any decisions or recommendations, as well as any briefing material (e.g., funding applications to support repatriation work to be carried out; other matters that may involve funding or program decisions by Council).

Both the Repatriation Committee and Council will be accountable to the Nation's members and will ensure timely, regular updates are provided to members. Council's communications department will work closely with the committee and consult members of the Nation to confirm best approaches for information sharing and updates.

Budget

The budget for the Repatriation Committee will be allocated by Council and will cover the following:

- Member honoraria
- Travel and transportation
- Research services
- Meeting space, note-taking, catering
- Printing and photocopying
- Communications
- Community meetings

Note: If Council applied for and received a Royal BC Museum Repatriation Grant, this can be noted here, and refer to the budget that was included with the grant application.

Goals

- Within two months, develop, finalize and implement committee policies, processes and procedures, including the administrative and operational resources required to maintain the committee's work.
- Within six months, develop a repatriation action plan that will see the return of our Ancestral remains and cultural belongings.
- Within two years, repatriate Ancestral remains from at least two museums and one post-secondary institution.
- Within five years, develop a plan and fundraising strategy to build a centre where repatriated cultural belongings can be housed.

Deliverables

An initial list of anticipated deliverables will be established at the committee's first meeting.

Sample Call for Proposals

In this example, the Repatriation Committee and community determined that a family history photo project would be important to initiate, to help families organize their respective photo collections to digitize and add to a new community photo history archive. This sample was created by Lou-ann Neel, repatriation specialist at the Royal BC Museum. The names and example are fictional and meant to serve only as samples or options for wording. It is an open-source document intended to be shared and used as a starting point for communities undertaking this type of work.

XYZ Nation, Indigenous Repatriation Committee
Family History Photo Project—Phase 1 of 4
REQUEST FOR PROPOSALS

Terminology

Indigenous Repatriation Committee is a group of 15 dedicated volunteers who provide recommendations to the leadership of the XYZ Nation for matters related to repatriation.

Family histories refers to the families of the XYZ Nation (a list will be provided with all relevant project information).

Repatriation refers to the return of our people's treasures and belongings—tangible and intangible—including Ancestral remains; burial belongings; individual, familial and tribal ceremonial and everyday cultural belongings; audio and video recordings; and standard and digital photographs.

Project team refers to the successful proponent (also referred to as respondent, bidder or applicant) to this request for proposals, along with designated members of the Indigenous Repatriation Committee.

The successful proponent will include a team of up to four individuals with demonstrated experience in working with First Nations communities, strong interpersonal skills, the ability to work independently, demonstrated experience in organizing photo collections, the ability to coordinate meetings and the ability to document notes for meetings.

Statement of Purpose

As part of its larger repatriation program, the XYZ Nation Indigenous Repatriation Committee has recently initiated the Family History Photo Project (Phase 1 of 4), which will help build a comprehensive photo archive of our community's history.

The Indigenous Repatriation Committee recognized that this photo archive would help each family affirm its history, connection to the tribe, and connection to our lands and waters, and help us to rebuild the parts of our culture that have been taken from us over the past 150+ years.

The committee also recognizes that it is important to involve all members of our Nation, whether they reside within our home communities or in urban centres, and whether they hold registered Indian status or not.

Background Information

The Indigenous Repatriation Committee is composed of 15 dedicated volunteers, including Elders, cultural knowledge-keepers, and family historians whose knowledge and experience have helped the XYZ Nation develop a repatriation plan that is now ready to implement.

The repatriation plan includes the Family History Photo Project, which will proceed simultaneously with several other important projects, including the Family Tree Project and Traditional Names Project. It is envisioned that these three projects will be intertwined, as they are each important aspects of our people's identity; but because of the volume of work that needs to be carried out, the committee felt it would be important for each project to have a dedicated team to ensure each project has the necessary attention and resources required for its success.

The first phase of the Family History Photo Project (Phase 1 of 4) is intended as a **planning and development phase**, where the project team will help families to organize their respective photo collections in preparation for digital scanning.

The project team will also assist in coordinating and documenting meetings within and between families, to discuss and determine which photos are to be included in the community photo archive, and which photos won't be part of the archive, but will still be digitized for the family.

1. Scope of Work

The goals for this project are to:

- Assist families in organizing their respective photo collections in preparation for digital scanning.
- Assist families and community members in coordinating meetings, taking notes, distributing notes and ensuring notes are submitted to the Indigenous Repatriation Committee.

The scope of work required will include:

- Meeting with designated members of the Indigenous Repatriation Committee to review the systems that will be used to organize family photo collections.
- Meeting with individuals and families to organize their photo collections.
- Coordinating and serving as note-taker for anywhere from four to six family or community meetings per month (for an estimated six months).

Roles and Responsibilities

The proponent will be responsible for:

- Using the systems developed by the Indigenous Repatriation Committee to begin organizing the photo collections of the XYZ Nation's members.
- Coordinating an initial series of community meetings to present an outline and timeline of the work they will be carrying out with members.
- Coordinating meetings with members to organize their photos.
- Preparing monthly reports for the Indigenous Repatriation Committee, and attending these meetings to present findings.

Project Timeline

The work will commence upon awarding of this contract. The duration of the contract is six months from the start of the contract (i.e., if the project commences on April 1, it will end on September 30).

2. RFP Procedures

Evaluation and Award Process

Proponents wishing to respond to this request for proposals must submit the following information to the committee:

- A cover letter introducing members of the team and explaining why the team is interested and best suited to the work outlined in the RFP (maximum two pages).
- Proponent's understanding of the project scope and approach; this can include examples of similar project work, including links to online examples (maximum four pages).
- Brief biographies for each team member (maximum one page each) describing how each member will contribute to the project.
- A minimum of three references (please briefly describe professional relationship with the reference and duration of the relationship).

Within one week (five business days) of the submission deadline, the Indigenous Repatriation Committee will review all submissions and select three proponents to be interviewed on (*day, month, year*).

These interviews will be 45 minutes in duration: 15 minutes for introductions and a project overview, 15 minutes for a presentation by the proponent and 15 minutes for any questions from the committee.

The committee will assess proponents on the following criteria and percentages:

- Demonstrated abilities in public speaking (25 per cent): Ability to engage an audience, confidence in speaking in public.

- Clarity of presentation: Proponent conveys their understanding of the project (25 per cent).
- Knowledge of how to organize photo collections (25 per cent).
- Report writing (25 per cent).

Process Schedule

The committee invites teams of Indigenous researchers (includes Indigenous post-secondary students at the graduate level), Indigenous freelance contractors with experience in organizing large photo collections (e.g., developing or maintaining a photo or document record system), and Indigenous professionals with experience working in First Nations community engagement, consultation, program and project development, implementation, delivery and evaluation.

All submissions must be in PDF format.

Please submit no more than 10 pages in total (i.e., as noted in Evaluation and Award Process above).

The committee reserves the right to request additional information if needed, acknowledging that this may result in changes to the dates provided in this RFP. Proponents will be notified of any changes or delays in the process.

Submissions will be accepted until 5:00 pm (*Pacific Standard Time*) (*day, month, year*) and must be submitted by email to:

ProjectManager@XYZNation.com

If the proponent is unable to send a submission by email, they should call the project manager at (123) 456-7891 to make alternate arrangements.

Submission Details

Any questions about the RFP, please contact the project manager at (123) 456-7891 or by email at ProjectManager@XYZNation.com.

3. RFP Submission Requirements

Proposal Format

- As noted in the Process Schedule section above, submissions must be in PDF format.
- Please submit no more than 10 pages in total (i.e., as noted in Process Schedule above).
- Page margins should be 1''. Font should be Arial 11 pt. The proponent's name should be in the header, and the page number in the footer.

References

Please provide a minimum of three references. References will be contacted only if the respondent completes the interview stage and is being strongly considered. The proponent should provide the following information for their references:

- Contact name and position
- Organization
- Telephone
- Email
- Description of the professional relationship with the reference and duration of the relationship

Note about Tax Status

By way of a formal submission to this RFP, proponents acknowledge and affirm their understanding that the successful proponent will not be an employee of the Indigenous Repatriation Committee or the XYZ Nation, but rather, an independent contractor, and as such, responsible for any taxes and other mandatory employment-related costs, including EI, WSBC, CPP, and personal and professional insurance.

Payment

- The total contract amount is $80,000 ($72,000 for fees; $8,000 for travel).
- Payments are based on a project schedule with terms and deliverables that will be finalized with the successful proponent upon award of the contract.

Termination of Agreement

- Consistent with the financial policies of the XYZ Nation, the contract may be terminated by the Indigenous Repatriation Committee or the proponent if there is an inability to complete the project or failure to deliver on the project schedule, terms or deliverables.

Limitations

- The XYZ Nation and its Indigenous Repatriation Committee declare that neither the issuing of this RFP nor receipt of a response to the RFP constitutes any form of contract or agreement with respect to the project.
- The committee reserves the right to cancel, amend or alter the RFP, its contents or the selection process.
- Since this RFP and the project it describes are fully dependent on the availability of project funding, the committee reserves the right to terminate any agreements or negotiation of agreements, should the applicable funding not be available.

Sample Oral History Release Form

To be read out loud by researcher and signed by the interviewee:

Project Overview

[*Provide clear, concise project overview*]

Interview Agreement

I ________________________________ agree to be interviewed for the purposes of [*project working title*] and in other educational or promotional projects related to this project as described above. My participation in this project is completely voluntary and I understand that:

- This interview will last up to [*xx*] hours, that it will be recorded [*type of recording, i.e., audio or audiovisual*] and transcribed in full.
- I do not have to answer any questions that I do not want to, and may stop the interview at any time.
- The copyright and intellectual property of this interview will remain my sole property.
- I will receive a raw copy of this interview and its transcript. Upon reviewing this material, I reserve the right to remove/change/correct any information I provided. I will receive a copy of both the final approved interview and its transcript.
- This interview may be edited for use in the [*project name*] in the form of a personal quote, longer text or as an [*audio or audiovisual recording*]. Any part of the recording and/or transcription (raw or edited) used for public consumption must be approved by me first.
- A copy of the final approved interview and transcript will be stored in the Haida Gwaii Museum Archives with research/public access as permitted below, unless otherwise stated.

  ☐ Keep a copy of the recording and/or transcript in the Haida Gwaii Museum Archives and make it accessible to the public.

- ☐ Keep a copy of the recording and/or transcript in the Haida Gwaii Museum Archives with restrictions on public access as follows: [*i.e., must contact interviewee for permission; or in the case of future access, permission must be given by a family member, etc.*]
- ☐ Other________________________________

- The museum's management of this interview and transcript will be in accordance with generally accepted principles of document conservation, which may include the destruction of certain documents and the conservation of all or part of the said archives by means of mechanical, photographic, and computerized process.
- My rate of pay for this interview will be: $[*xx*]/hour.

Location and date of interview: ____________________________

Participant name: ____________________________
Participant signature: ____________________________
Mailing address: ____________________________
____
Phone: ____________________________
Email: ____________________________
Date: ____________________________

Interviewer's name: ____________________________
Interviewer's signature: ____________________________
Date: ____________________________

APPENDIX D

Fundraising Resources

Grant Agencies

BC Alliance for Arts + Culture Calendar of grant agencies at a glance

allianceforarts.com/grants

Bill Holm Center at the Burke Museum

burkemuseum.org/research-and-collections/bill-holm-center/grants

BC Arts Council

bcartscouncil.ca/deadlines_date.html

Canada Council for the Arts

canadacouncil.ca/funding/grants/creating-knowing-sharing

Canadian Heritage Aboriginal Heritage Museums Assistance Program

canada.ca/en/canadian-heritage/services/funding/museums-assistance/aboriginal-heritage.html (bit.ly/HeritageMAP)

Canadian Heritage Aboriginal Peoples Program

canada.ca/en/canadian-heritage/services/funding/aboriginal-peoples.html

First Peoples' Cultural Council

fpcc.ca/arts/Programs

fpcc.ca/culture/projects

Friends of the BC Archives
friendsofbcarchives.wordpress.com/indigenous-research-fund

Heritage BC
heritagebc.ca/heritage-legacy-fund

Indigitization
indigitization.ca/grant-program

Royal British Columbia Museum
Repatriation Grant
royalbcmuseum.bc.ca/first-nations/first-nations-repatriation/grant

Smithsonian Institution
Recovering Voices Community Research Grant
recoveringvoices.si.edu/resourcesandgrants/grants.html

Young Canada Works
Summer students and interns
canada.ca/en/canadian-heritage/services/
funding/young-canada-works.html

YVR Arts Foundation
Masterpiece Study Program Grants
yvraf.com/programs/masterpiece-study-program-grants

Grant Writing Tips

There are many different grant programs available to individuals, groups and organizations. Grants can be found at local, municipal, regional, provincial, national and international levels, and can support a wide range of activities.

Each grant program has a program description that lets you know what types of projects will be considered for funding, along with information on things that won't be considered for funding. The program descriptions will also tell you about the funding agency's priorities and their vision.

Before you start, there are four things to keep in mind:

1. *Match Your Idea with a Grant Program*

Find a grant program to fit your idea rather than trying to create a new idea that fits into an existing grant program. Often, people will hear about a grant or the grant deadline and attempt to create a new idea at the last possible minute. Not only is this stressful, it often doesn't work.

Instead, take the time to focus on what you really want to do. Put your ideas and thoughts to paper; elaborate on some of the logistics such as who, what, where, when, how and why; THEN have a look at the funders to see which ones are the closest match to your idea.

Once you identify a funder that looks like a match for your project idea, give them a call or email them to see if you are eligible to apply and to get any feedback, advice or guidance on how to proceed with your application.

2. *Leave Yourself a Lot of Time*

Grant writing takes time, so don't leave it to the last minute—you want to give yourself the best chance at being awarded a grant—and that simply takes time.

The more time you have, the better: a month before the deadline is ideal, as you'll need time for yourself and others to review your application package.

3. Create a Grant-Writing Calendar

Creating your own grant-writing calendar will enable you to schedule quality blocks of time you can spend thinking and sketching out your project ideas.

You can put grant deadlines onto your regular calendar or day-timer, or set up a calendar in your email program (such as Outlook) or through an online calendar such as Google's.

Having a birds-eye view of grant deadlines for the year will help you to decide which grants you want to apply for and help you to get organized in gathering the information you'll need for each one.

4. Use Creative, Flexible and Adaptable Approaches

Along with a grant-writing calendar, it's also good to think about the approaches you can take to complete the goals you and/or your community have established. For instance, mapping out your project ideas in shorter phases (e.g., things that can be reasonably accomplished within a one-year period) versus a longer project that would require multi-year funding, is a creative, flexible and adaptable approach that will enable your community and project team to proceed with the proposed project in manageable pieces.

For example, if you have a project that involves digitizing audio cassettes so they can be transcribed, translated and then made into language learning resources, you could create this as a project with four phases:

- Phase 1: Digitize audio cassettes into MP3 and WAV formats.
- Phase 2: Transcribe digitized audio into (*your Indigenous language*).
- Phase 3: Translate into English and/or another language.
- Phase 4: Use digital audio, translations and transcriptions to create new language learning materials and resources.

Since most grant programs require projects to start and finish within a one-year period, the multi-phase approach enables the important work to be carried out within those timelines, and it helps you to see whether the level of funding is fairly and equitably distributed across all tasks and to each member of the project team.

And finally, most grant application packages now include a checklist at the back of the application package that will help you to plan for things like letters of support, work plans and quotes for specific budget items. For example, the Royal BC Museum Repatriation Grant Program application package includes the following checklist:

Royal BC Museum Repatriation Grant Program Checklist

- A fully completed and signed **application form** (including this checklist).
- A detailed **timeline** describing all project activities, who will be involved, and anticipated outcomes or deliverables.
- **CVs, resumes and/or biographies** for all key participants, and how each relates to or contributes to the proposed project.
- A **project budget**, which details all anticipated expenses and revenues from all sources.
- **Notification dates** for unconfirmed resources.
- A **letter from the museum** or institution confirming their commitment to the repatriation project.
- Two current **letters of support** specifically for this applicant and proposal.
- If applicant is a Band Council, include a **band council resolution** or letter from the Tribal office or band council confirming their support of the application and their commitment to the repatriation project and designating the contact person for the project. If the applicant is a not-for-profit society, include a **Board Resolution** confirming their support of the application and their commitment to the repatriation project and designating the contact person for the project.

One way to get things organized is to use the following project planning template to share with those who will be involved in the proposed project, including those who you will be asking to provide letters of support for the application. This will provide an opportunity for all participants to provide feedback to the proposed project, and to provide letters of support and other materials that relate directly to the project. It is also a good way for you to move from a brief elevator-pitch description of your project idea to a birds-eye view of the realistic timelines and key milestones you hope to achieve.

The project-planning template can be customized to suit your project: simply add columns with the appropriate headings. Some find it useful to create the plan within a spreadsheet such as Excel to enable actual budget amounts to be included. This can make it much easier to align actions with actual costs and any in-kind contributions, and to create a cash-flow sheet that will be handy once the project is ready to implement.

And finally, the template can help you to create an illustrated flowchart that can be used to provide updates to community members. This can be in the form of a graphic to include with each newsletter, a large poster display in various buildings in the community, and on the Nation's website, with interactive areas that provide more detail on accomplishments and plans.

Project Planning Template

Proposed Project: Establishment of a Repatriation Committee
Anticipated Timeline: April 1–May 31
Purpose: For the Repatriation Committee to develop an action plan that will guide each step of our Nation's repatriation process, and to implement the portions of the plan that can be accomplished within the stated timeline.

Table 4.
Project planning template.

DATE	WHO	WHAT	WHERE	WHEN	HOW	BUDGET
April 1	Project manager	Coordinate community gathering to discuss & form a Repatriation Committee	Council hall	By April 30	Written invitations Verbal invitations Web Posters	Project manager fee Printing Catering Event staff Local transportation
April 15	Project manager	Coordinate Repatriation Committee's first meeting Prep all info in Terms of Reference that need to be discussed and finalized	Council hall or Elders' centre	By April 30	Book meeting space & catering Contact all members appointed at community gathering Provide meeting package to each Host meeting	Protocol Meeting space Catering Printing Local transportation Admin support: meeting notes, summary of decisions
May 1	Project manager	Schedule all committee meeting dates with members	Confirm locations for each meeting	By May 15	Schedule facilities, any equipment, materials, catering, transportation and admin support services for all meetings	Provide all projected costs to finance manager

APPENDIX E

Sample Letters to Museums

Nowadays, whether making initial contact with museums or arranging visits or repatriations, communication is largely done by email, phone or in person, but it is important to document the work of repatriation by keeping records as well—for both museums and your own community. Starting next page are three sample letters, keeping in mind that repatriations work differently for different Nations and museums. They also give an example of two communities and two organizations within one Nation working together on repatriation.

First Peoples gallery, RBCM: close-up of the model village of Skedans, a Haida village. Photo courtesy Lou-ann Neel.

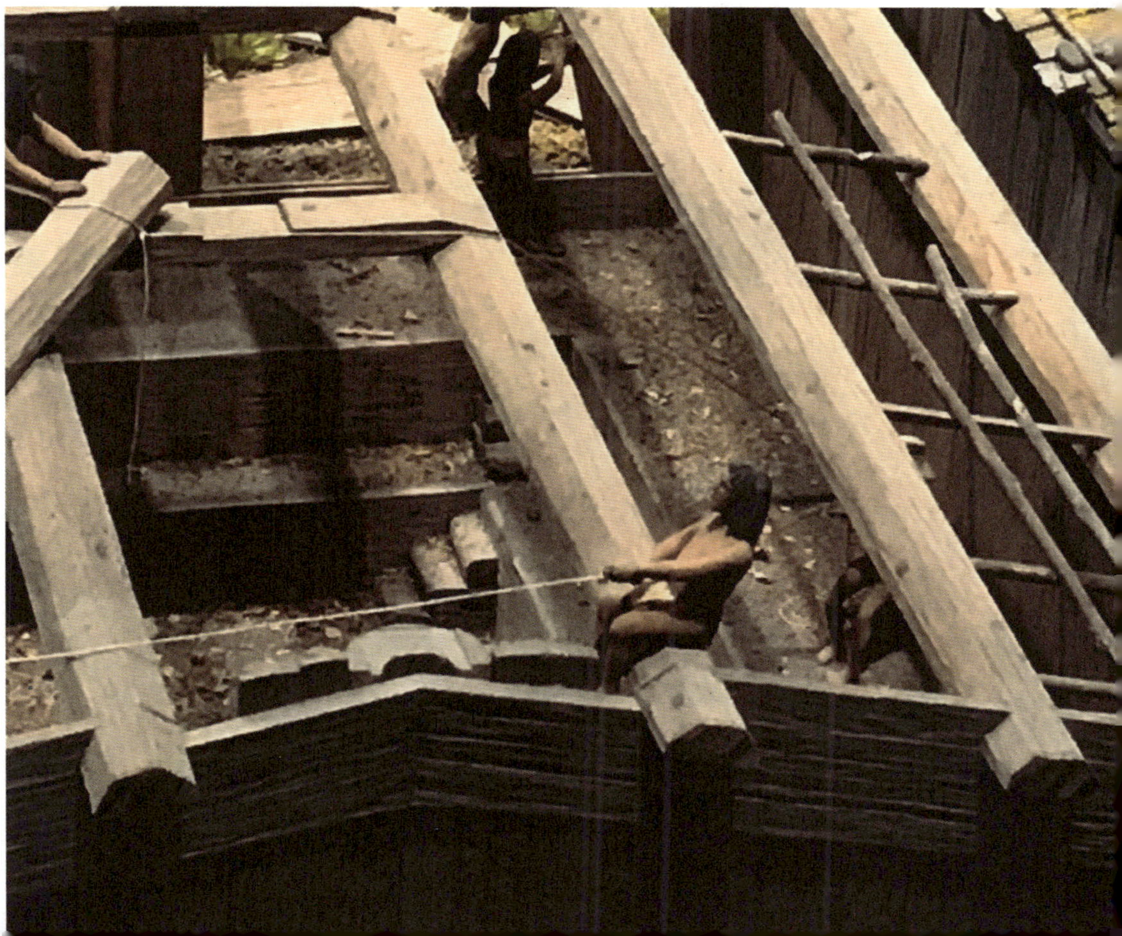

Sample Letter: Locating Your Ancestors and Belongings

August 15, 2020

__________, Head of Repatriation
The Museum of Museums
123 Main Street
Ottawa, Ontario A1B 2C3

RE: Research request

Dear __________,

We hope this letter finds you well. The Haida Nation is researching its cultural heritage held in museums around the world. We are writing on behalf of the Haida Nation to request a complete inventory of human remains and cultural objects that are attributed to our Nation or collected in our territory.

For your records, please find attached a letter from our leaders, authorizing our organizations to conduct this work on behalf of the Haida Nation. Should you have any questions, please do not hesitate to contact us.

Sincerely,

Nika Collison
Executive Director,
Haida Gwaii Museum
Co-Chair, Haida Repatriation Committee
Skidegate Branch
p. 123-456-5555 xt. 111
e. lookoutherewecome@internet.com

Vince Collison
Repatriation Dept., Old Massett Heritage Resources
Co-Chair, Haida Repatriation Committee
Old Massett Branch
p. 123-456-4444
e. repatriationnation@12345.ca

cc: President, Haida Nation

Council of the Haida Nation

February 23, 2000

To Whom It May Concern:

Please be advised that the **Old Massett & Skidegate Repatriation Committees** are authorized to undertake the repatriation of Haida ancestral remains and cultural objects from museums and other institutions around the world. The committees work through Old Massett Heritage Resources and the Haida Gwaii Museum respectfully, supervising any repatriation undertakings.

The Haida Nation sees repatriation as based upon mutual respect, co-operation and trust between the Haida and the museum community. The matter of repatriation is not viewed by the Haida Nation as the substance of Treaty Negotiations. Consequently, the return of Haida ancestral remains and cultural objects from museums/institutions to Haida Gwaii should not be subject to the finalization of a treaty process.

As the Haida Nation, we accept our responsibility to ensure that our Haida heritage endures from our past, through today and into the future; repatriation is a part of that responsibility.

We the undersigned support the **Old Massett & Skidegate Repatriation Committees** in their continued work to build good relationships with museums and institutions around the world and to bring home Haida ancestral remains and cultural objects.

Respectfully,

signatures on following pages

☐ Box 98 Skidegate, Haida Gwaii V0T 1S1 • Phone (250) 559-4468 • Fax (250) 559-8951

☐ Box 589 Massett, Haida Gwaii V0T 1M0 • Phone (250) 626-5252 • Fax (250) 626-3403

Sample Letter: Viewing Collections and Archives

January 10, 2021

__________, Head of Repatriation
The Museum of Museums
123 Main Street
Ottawa, Ontario A1B 2C3

RE: Research visit, June 2021

Dear __________,

Please accept this letter as the official notice of our travels to the Museum of Museums from June 8 to 11, 2021, with a 20-person delegation.

As agreed, we will be visiting our Ancestors and cultural heritage held in your museum with the following provided by the Museum of Museums during our visit:

- ☐ One wheelchair for an Elder while at the museum
- ☐ A private space for ceremony (including smudging), rest and food breaks
- ☐ An outdoor area to conduct food burnings

Haawa—thank you for your assistance in arranging this visit. We look forward to working with you and your team. Should you have any questions, please do not hesitate to contact us.

Sincerely,

Nika Collison
Executive Director,
Haida Gwaii Museum
Co-Chair, Haida Repatriation Committee
Skidegate Branch
p. 123-456-5555 xt. 111
e. lookoutherewecome@internet.com

Vince Collison
Repatriation Dept., Old Massett Heritage Resources
Co-Chair, Haida Repatriation Committee
Old Massett Branch
p. 123-456-4444
e. repatriationnation@12345.ca

cc: President, Haida Nation

Sample Letter: Repatriation Official Request

September 14, 2021

_________, Head of Repatriation
The Museum of Museums
123 Main Street
Toronto, Ontario A1B 2C3

RE: Repatriation of Ancestors

Dear _________,

Please accept this letter as the Haida Nation's official request for the repatriation of our Ancestors and associated burial goods from the Museum of Museums this fall as detailed below:

"Queen Charlotte Islands" (Haida Gwaii), location unknown
11/123—1 rib fragment
12/123—3 pelvic bones

"Queen Charlotte Islands" (Haida Gwaii), Village of Old Town
13/123—1 femur
14/123—1 copper bracelet

As we discussed, a 25-person delegation will be travelling to your museum to prepare our Ancestors for their journey home between November 10 and 15, 2021, as well as to visit our collection of treasures again. As agreed, the following will be provided by your museum for this repatriation:

- ☐ $1,234 toward the cost of transporting our Ancestors
- ☐ Three wheelchairs for Elders while at the museum
- ☐ Unbleached cotton or muslin cloth to wrap our Ancestors
- ☐ Cedar chips for packing
- ☐ A private room to prepare our Ancestors for their journey home (smudging may be involved)

- ☐ A private space for ceremony (including smudging), rest and food breaks
- ☐ An outdoor area to conduct food burnings
- ☐ A space for a Yahguudangang—To Pay Respect ceremony and sharing of food with museum staff to officiate the transfer of our Ancestors under Haida legal traditions

As also agreed, the following items from our collection will be used in ceremony during the Yahguudangang—To Pay Respect feast:

- ☐ Copper—Nb1.123
- ☐ Bentwood chest—Nb1.234 1/2
- ☐ Rattle—Nb1.345
- ☐ Eagle Woman mask—Nb1.456

We understand that the headdress we requested to use (Nb1.567) in ceremony is not stable enough to be worn. We request it still be present during the feast. We can discuss what this might look like during our next phone call.

Haawa—thank you to you and your team for all the work you've done to assist us with this repatriation. We look forward to visiting with you and the rest of your team. Should you have any questions, please do not hesitate to contact us.

Sincerely,

Nika Collison
Executive Director,
Haida Gwaii Museum
Co-Chair, Haida Repatriation Committee
Skidegate Branch
p. 123-456-5555 xt. 111
e. lookoutherewecome@internet.com

Vince Collison
Repatriation Dept., Old Massett Heritage Resources
Co-Chair, Haida Repatriation Committee
Old Massett Branch
p. 123-456-4444
e. repatriationnation@12345.ca

cc: President, Haida Nation

APPENDIX F

Tips for Planning for Travel and Transport

Logistics, logistics, logistics! When travelling to a museum, there can be a lot of planning involved with the host museum and with your travels, especially if you are bringing your Ancestors or cultural heritage home.

Organizing with Museums

When organizing with museums, there is much to consider. Each Nation and museum will prepare in a manner that works best for their situation, but here are some things to think about when you plan together:

- Do you need space(s) for the following?
  - food burnings
  - smudging
  - preparing Ancestors for their journey home
  - breaks and nourishment
  - legalizing the repatriation through Indigenous laws or protocols, i.e., feasting, ceremony, or whatever way your Nation conducts business (there will be a legal transfer document the museum will require to be signed by both parties, as well)
- How will you and/or your delegation and museum staff get to know each other before getting into your work?
- What needs do Elders and others requiring assistance have (e.g., wheelchairs)?
- How will you secure accommodation close to the museum?

- How will you organize transport from your accommodations to the museum and back, if needed?
- Seasons and the weather: what type of climate will you be in? Are the temperatures extreme compared to home? What clothing and other gear will be best suited to stay comfortable while visiting?
- If you are transporting large or multiple containers home by air, how will they be transported to the airport, and from the plane back to your community?
- Will you have the opportunity to meet with, gift and thank the Indigenous Nation on whose territory the museum exists?
- Have you thoroughly reviewed your community's protocols with the museum, and has the museum thoroughly reviewed their protocols with you? Are negotiations or adaptations needed on either or both ends?
- Are you interested in sharing in some of your culture with the general public (i.e., traditional song/dance, presentations, art demonstrations)? This can be a great way to educate the public about your Nation and ways of life.
- Does the museum have funding or in-kind support they can contribute to your expenses?
- Have you considered inviting museum staff to your community for the reburial or repatriation event?

Working with the Canadian Consulate

If you are bringing someone or something home from another country, contact the Canadian consulate office well in advance! Involving the Canadian consulate is very important when nation-state borders are involved. They can advise on travel considerations in foreign countries, help establish relationships with museums and make cross-border travel smooth—such as helping with travel logistics for individuals and groups and what the travellers might be bringing with them that could become problematic at the border (e.g., traditional foods, eagle feathers, certain furs, etc.). They can also help with arranging to bring your Ancestors and belongings home through border and airport security, so you don't get held up trying to explain why you are transporting human remains or historical cultural objects.

To learn more or to contact the Canadian consulate and their services, visit:
travel.gc.ca/assistance/emergency-info/consular/canadian-consular-services-charter

Getting a Passport

For cross-border travel, you need a passport. For those who have status cards, you may be able to use these to get into and out of the United States by land, but it's still highly recommended to get yourself a passport. You will definitely need one for travel outside of North America. While 24-hour passports can be acquired, it's better not to gamble: apply for your passport at *least* a month before your travel date.
canada.ca/en/immigration-refugees-citizenship/services/canadian-passports.html

Travelling by Airplane

If you are bringing Ancestral remains and belongings home, or travelling cross-border with food, eagle feathers, furs, etc., let the airline know well in advance as well, so they are aware of and ready for your journey. This is as important as contacting the Canadian consulate. If everyone knows what's happening in advance, the trip will go much more smoothly.

Airlines can be very helpful with group travel, as well as to arrange wheelchair/transport service at the airport if needed. It is also critical that they know if you're bringing home Ancestors and the volume of the transport containers. Are the transport containers small enough to travel on the plane with you, or do they have to go in the cargo compartment? Airlines can also help with sensitivities around loading and unloading the cargo compartment, if that is how transport needs to occur.

Ask the airline to help make sure airport security is also aware of your travels. If you are bringing your Ancestors' remains or cultural treasures on the plane with you, they might not have to go through the scanning process at security if they know in advance. If they don't have to go through a scanner, be prepared that security will still have to inspect what you are carrying with you.

Depending on the airline, you may find support that goes beyond logistical assistance. It doesn't hurt to ask airlines to waive fees or reduce costs for transporting your Ancestors. Some airlines bring their own respectful traditions for transporting the deceased. For example, when the Haida were bringing home Ancestors with an Asian-owned airline, the airline asked if the Haida could have their Ancestors facing in the same direction, and to mark their travel containers so the airline could ensure the Ancestors were facing the same direction as the other passengers while travelling on the plane.

General Checklist for Travel

- If travelling cross-border: Canadian consulate has been contacted for assistance.
- If travelling cross-border: Everyone has their passport (make sure to leave a photocopy of your passport with a trusted individual at home and give one to a travel partner just in case you lose yours on the road).
- If travelling in Canada, everyone has a valid piece of ID.
- Airline has been contacted to advise them of your travel and ask for assistance.
- You know the airline's maximum weight and size for carry-on luggage.

- Any logistical support required for Elders or others requiring assistance has been communicated to the Canadian consulate, airlines and the museum(s) you are visiting.
- Indigenous Nations of the territory you are visiting are aware of your pending visit (museums can assist with this).
- Hotels or other accommodation are booked.
- Per diems are in place for delegates.
- Travel insurance has been secured for people and their regalia or other cultural belongings travelling with the delegation.
- Each person in the delegation has copies of all pertinent travel information (i.e., plane tickets, itinerary, and emergency numbers such as the consulate and primary museum contact, cell phone numbers of others travelling, etc.).
- A list of the travellers and a copy of their itineraries, etc., is also kept at home in case of emergency.
- A buddy system has been assigned.

APPENDIX G

Global Museums with Major Indigenous Collections from BC

Museums come in many forms, such as community and regional museums, university museums, public art museums and galleries, and government-owned or -funded museums, to name a few. Many of them hold Indigenous Ancestral remains from around the world; most hold an astonishing amount of tangible and intangible Indigenous cultural heritage as well. Visit Part 5: Repatriation from Other Institutions for an overview of the different approaches, laws and guidelines some countries are adopting to address repatriation. National or state museums are usually bound to their government's legislation and may also have institutional policies. University museums are similar in that they are bound to higher-level university policy but also have internal policies. Museums that operate independently from government will have their own institutional policies.

The following provides information on some of the global museums holding larger known collections of Indigenous Ancestral remains or cultural treasures of Indigenous Peoples from BC. The resources provided are based on information available during the production of this handbook. Keep in mind that not all museums listed are guaranteed to hold Ancestral remains or cultural heritage from each Indigenous community in BC.

Also keep in mind that there may be other museums that hold Indigenous Ancestral remains and cultural heritage beyond what is included in this handbook. With so many museums in the world, there is a lot more information to gather, including the Indigenous territories museums are located on. We have provided this information where possible, but not every museum in North America has begun to make territorial acknowledgements, or they are still working with local Indigenous communities to determine the proper acknowledgement.

This handbook will be revised on an annual basis to update existing information and provide additional information on museums as it is gathered. While the resources in this handbook will get you familiarized with some of the collections that museums hold and their approaches to repatriation, the best way to find out who these museums are and what they do is to contact them directly.

Another handy resource is the UBC Reciprocal Research Network, which provides information on and images of Indigenous cultural items held at dozens of institutions. It is a great place to get an idea of what might be out there!
www.rrncommunity.org

Canada

Library and Archives Canada

For an overview of the collection held at Library and Archives Canada, visit:
bac-lac.gc.ca/eng/about-us/about-collection/Pages/about.aspx

Library and Archives Canada
395 Wellington Street
Ottawa, ON K1A 0N4
Phone: (613) 996-5115 or
(866) 578-7777 (toll free)
General inquiries (email):
www.bac-lac.gc.ca/eng/assistance-request-form/Pages/assistance-request-form.aspx?requesttype=3 (bit.ly/LACquestion)

Vancouver Office
Library Square Tower
420 – 300 West Georgia Street
Vancouver, BC V6B 6B4
Phone: (604) 666-9699

Indigenous Heritage Search
bac-lac.gc.ca/eng/discover/aboriginal-heritage/pages/introduction.aspx (bit.ly/LACIndigenous)

General Collections Search
bac-lac.gc.ca/eng/about-us/about-collection/Pages/about.aspx

Indigenous Advisory Circle
bac-lac.gc.ca/eng/about-us/Pages/Indigenous-Advisory-Circle.aspx

Alberta

Glenbow Museum

Blackfoot territory

For an overview of the collections held at the Glenbow Museum, visit: glenbow.org/collections/museum/native

Address
Glenbow Museum
130 – 9 Avenue SE
Calgary, Alberta T2G 0P3
Phone: (403) 268-4101
Email: info@glenbow.org
Contacts page: glenbow.org/contact.cfm
glenbow.org/index.cfm

Archives Contact
Kim Geraldi, Librarian
Library reference desk: (403) 268-4197
Library email: library@glenbow.org

Collections Contacts
Daryl Betenia
Manager, Collections
Phone: (403) 268-4238
Email: dbetenia@glenbow.org

Joanne Schmidt
Curator of Indigenous Studies
Native North America Collections
Phone: (403) 268-4176
Email: jschmidt@glenbow.org

Collections Search
glenbow.org/collections/search

Glenbow-Alberta Institute Act
qp.alberta.ca/documents/Acts/G06.pdf

Heritage Division Collections Management Policy
provincialarchives.alberta.ca/docs/who-we-are/about-us/opman/CollectionsPolicy.pdf (bit.ly/UAcollections)

First Nations Sacred Ceremonial Objects Repatriation Act
qp.alberta.ca/1266.cfm?page=F14.cfm&leg_type=Acts&isbncln=9780779794331 (bit.ly/FNSCO)

The effects of repatriation on the relationship between the Glenbow Museum and the Blackfoot people
tandfonline.com/doi/pdf/10.1080/09647770802234037

British Columbia

City of Vancouver Archives

xʷməθkʷəy̓əm (Musqueam), Sḵwx̱wú7mesh (Squamish), səlilwətaɬ (Tsleil-Waututh) territory

Address
City of Vancouver Archives
1150 Chestnut Street
Vancouver, BC V6J 3J9
Phone: (604) 736-8561
Email: archives@vancouver.ca
vancouver.ca/your-government/city-of-vancouver-archives.aspx

Collections Search
searcharchives.vancouver.ca

Museum of Vancouver

xʷməθkʷəy̓əm (Musqueam), səl̓ilwətaʔɬ (Tsleil-Waututh) and Sḵwx̱wú7mesh (Squamish) territory

For an overview of collections held at the Museum of Vancouver, visit: museumofvancouver.ca/museum-collection-and-openmov

Address
Museum of Vancouver
1100 Chestnut Street
Vancouver, BC V6J 3J9
Phone: (604) 736-4431
Contacts page:
museumofvancouver.ca/contact-us

Collections Contact
Sharon Fortney
Curator of Indigenous Collections and Engagement
Phone: (604) 730-5301
Email:
sfortney@museumofvancouver.ca

Collections Search
openmov.museumofvancouver.ca/collection

Royal British Columbia Museum

Lekwungen territory (Songhees/Esquimalt (xwsepsum) Nations)

See Part 4: Repatriation from the Royal BC Museum of this handbook for detailed information.

Territory
Lekwungen Territories
Songhees Nation
1100 Admirals Road
Victoria, BC V9A 2P6
Phone: (250) 386-1043
songheesnation.ca

Esquimalt Nation
1189 Kosapsum Road
Victoria, BC V9A 7K7
(250) 381-7861
esquimaltnation.ca

Address
Royal British Columbia Museum
675 Belleville Street
Victoria, BC V8W 9W2
Phone: (250) 356-7226 or
(888) 447-7977 (toll free)
rbcm.ca

Simon Fraser University Bill Reid Centre

xʷməθkʷəy̓əm (Musqueam), Sḵwx̱wú7mesh (Squamish), səl̓ílwətaʔɬ (Tsleil-Waututh), and the kʷikʷəƛ̓əm (Kwikwetlem) territory

For an overview of the collection held at SFU Bill Reid Centre, visit:
sfu.ca/brc/objective.html

Address
SFU Bill Reid Centre
Department of First Nations Studies
SWH 9091, 8888 University Drive
Burnaby, BC V5A 1S6
Phone: (778) 782-9882
Email: brctr@sfu.ca
sfu.ca/brc.html

Digitized Collections Search
digital.lib.sfu.ca/billreid-collection/bill-reid-centre-collection

Simon Fraser University Museum of Archaeology and Ethnology

xʷməθkʷəy̓əm (Musqueam), Sḵwx̱wú7mesh (Squamish), səl̓ílwətaʔɬ (Tsleil-Waututh), and the kʷikʷəƛ̓əm (Kwikwetlem) territory

For an overview of collections held at the SFU Museum of Archaeology and Ethnology, visit:
sfu.ca/archaeology/museum/about.html

Address
Simon Fraser University Museum of Archaeology and Ethnology
Saywell Hall
8888 University Drive
Burnaby, BC V5A 1S6
Phone: (778) 782-3135
General inquiries (email):
sfu.ca/archaeology/museum/contact.html

Contact
Dr. Barbara J. Winter
Director
Phone: (778) 782-3325
Email: museum@sfu.ca

sfu.ca/archaeology/museum.html

Getting Involved with the Museum
sfu.ca/archaeology/museum/getting-involved.html

UBC Laboratory of Archaeology

xʷməθkʷəy̓əm (Musqueam) territory

For an overview of collections held at the UBC Laboratory of Archaeology, visit:
anth.ubc.ca/research/laboratory-of-archaeology

Address
UBC Laboratory of Archaeology
6303 NW Marine Drive
Vancouver, BC V6T 1Z1
Phone: (604) 822-2878
anth.ubc.ca/research/laboratory-of-archaeology

Repatriation Contact
Andrew Martindale, Director
Phone: (604) 822-3124
Email: andrew.martindale@ubc.ca

Repatriation Guidelines
anth.ubc.ca/research/laboratory-of-archaeology/repatriation-guidelines-for-first-nations (bit.ly/UBCrepatriation)

UBC Museum of Anthropology

xʷməθkʷəy̓əm (Musqueam) territory

For an overview of collections held at the UBC Museum of Anthropology, visit:
moa.ubc.ca
under Research & Collections.

Address
UBC Museum of Anthropology
6393 NW Marine Drive
Vancouver, BC V6T 1Z2
Phone: (604) 822-5087
moa.ubc.ca

Repatriation Contact
Sue Rowley, Repatriation Committee Chair
Phone: (604) 822-5087
Email: susan.rowley@ubc.ca

Archives Contact
Audrey and Harry Hawthorn Library and Archives
Alissa Cherry, Research Manager
Phone: (604) 822-4834
Email: library@moa.ubc.ca

Collections Contact
Heidi Swierenga, Department Head Collections Care and Access
Phone: (604) 822-5087
Email: heidi.swierenga@ubc.ca
General inquiries: objects@moa.ubc.ca

Collections Search
collection-online.moa.ubc.ca

Archives Search
atom.moa.ubc.ca/index.php

Library Search
webcat1.library.ubc.ca:7108/vwebv/search?searchCode=GKEY%5e*&limitTo=LOCA=Museum+of+Anthropology+Reading+Room (bit.ly/UBCkeyword)

Additional Research: The Reciprocal Research Network, a central database containing information on collections held in dozens of institutions
rrncommunity.org

Repatriation Guidelines
moa.ubc.ca/wp-content/uploads/2014/09/Resources-Repatriation-Guidelines.pdf

Repatriation Policy "Deaccession of Works of Art and/or Cultural Materials"
universitycounsel.ubc.ca/files/2018/09/policy128.pdf

Repatriation Teaching Kit: Returning the Past: Repatriation of First Nations Cultural Property
moa.ubc.ca/wp-content/uploads/TeachingKit-Repatriation.pdf

Ontario

Royal Ontario Museum

For an overview of collections held at the Royal Ontario Museum, visit:
rom.on.ca/en/collections-research

Address
Royal Ontario Museum
100 Queens Park
Toronto, ON M5S 2C6
Phone: (416) 586-8000
rom.on.ca/en

Collections Contact
Craig N. Cipolla
Associate Curator of North American Archaeology
Email (scroll to bottom of webpage to access):
rom.on.ca/en/collections-research/rom-staff/craig-n-cipolla

Archives Contact
Charlotte Chaffey
Archives/Records Manager
Phone: (416) 586-5596
Email (scroll to bottom of webpage to access):
rom.on.ca/en/collections-research/rom-staff/charlotte-chaffey

Collections Search
rom.on.ca/en/collections-research/online-collections

Repatriation of Human Remains of the Aboriginal Peoples of Canada Policy
rom.on.ca/sites/default/files/imce/hrrepatriationtrev2012.pdf

Repatriation of Canadian Aboriginal Objects Policy
rom.on.ca/sites/default/files/imce/RepatriationCAOREV2012_0.pdf

Quebec

Canadian Museum of History

Kitigan Zibi, Anishinabeg of Algonquin territory

For an overview of collections held at the Canadian Museum of History, visit:
historymuseum.ca/learn/resource-centre

Address
Canadian Museum of History
100 Laurier Street
Gatineau, QC K1A 0M8
Phone: (819) 776-7000 or
(800) 555-5621 (toll free)
historymuseum.ca

Collections Contact
Wanda McWilliams
Director, Collections Management and Conservation
Phone: (819) 776-8434
Email:
wanda.mcwilliams@historymuseum.ca

Indigenous Relations Officer
Jameson C. Brant
Phone: (819) 776-7180
Email:
Jameson.Brant@
historymuseum.ca

Repatriation Contact
Nadja Roby
Manager, Repatriation and
Indigenous Relations
Phone: (819) 776-8440
Email: Nadja.Roby@historymuseum.ca

Online Collections Search
historymuseum.ca/collections

Online Repatriation Information
historymuseum.ca/learn/research/repatriation/#tabs

Online Repatriation Policy
historymuseum.ca/wp-content/uploads/2015/09/
REPATRIATION-POLICY.pdf

Evidence—CHPC (42-1)—No. 122—House of Commons of Canada
Re: Bill C-391, An act respecting a national strategy for
the repatriation of Aboriginal cultural property
ourcommons.ca/DocumentViewer/en/42
-1/CHPC/meeting-122/evidence

Training Opportunities
RBC Indigenous Internship Program
Gaëlle Mollen
Coordinator, Indigenous Internship Program
Phone: (819) 776-8270
Email: gaelle.mollen@historymuseum.ca

McCord Museum of Canadian History

For an overview of collections held at the McCord Museum, visit:
musee-mccord.qc.ca/en/collections/indigenous-cultures

Address
McCord Museum
690 Sherbrooke Street West
Montreal, QC H3A 1E9
Phone: (514) 861-6701
General inquiries: info.mccord@mccord-stewart.ca

List of Museum Staff
musee-mccord.qc.ca/en/museum-staff

Collections Search
collections.musee-mccord.qc.ca/en/keys/collections

United States of America

Illinois

Field Museum

Three Fires Confederacy: Ojibwe, Odawa, and Potawatomi territory
For an overview of collections held at the Field Museum, visit:
fieldmuseum.org/science/research/area/cultures-north-america

Address
1400 South Lake Shore Drive
Chicago, IL 60605
USA
Phone: (312) 992-9410
fieldmuseum.org

Collections Contact
Alaka Wali
Curator of North American Anthropology
Email: awali@fieldmuseum.org

Repatriation Contact
Helen Robbins
Repatriation Director
Phone: (312) 665-7317
Email: hrobbins@fieldmuseum.org

Collections Search
collections-anthropology.fieldmuseum.org/node?page=3

Access to Collections Policy
collections-anthropology.fieldmuseum.org/sites/
collections-anthropology.fieldmuseum.org/files/Visit%20
Policies%20and%20Procedures.pdf (bit.ly/FieldAccess)

Massachusetts

Peabody Essex Museum

For an overview of collections held at the Peabody Essex Museum, visit:
pem.org/explore-art/native-american-art

Address
Peabody Essex Museum
161 Essex Street
Salem, MA 01970
USA
Phone: (978) 745-9500
General inquiries: information@pem.org
pem.org

Collections Contact
Email: pem_collection@pem.org

Curator of Native American and Oceanic Art and Culture
pem.org/about-pem/curators/karen-kramer-curator-of-native-american-and-oceanic-art-and-culture (bit.ly/KarenKramer)

Collections Access Request
formstack.com/forms/pem-collection_access_request (bit.ly/CollectionAccess)

Native American Fellowship Program
pem.org/employment/native-american-fellowship-program/about-our--program (bit.ly/PEMabout)

Peabody Museum of Archaeology and Ethnology

For an overview of collections held in the Peabody Museum of Archaeology and Ethnology, visit: peabody.harvard.edu/collections

Address
Peabody Museum of Archaeology and Ethnology
Harvard University
11 Divinity Avenue
Cambridge, MA 02138
USA
Phone: (617) 496-1027
peabody.harvard.edu

List of Staff Departments
peabody.harvard.edu/node/237

Collections Search
https://pmem.unix.fas.harvard.edu:8443/peabody

Repatriation Overview
peabody.harvard.edu/node/310

Repatriation Contacts and Forms
peabody.harvard.edu/node/591

New York

American Museum of Natural History

Lenape territory

For an overview of collections held at the American Museum of Natural History, view: amnh.org/our-research/anthropology/collections

Address
Central Park West at 79th Street
New York, NY 10024-5192
USA
Phone: (212) 769-5100
amnh.org

Collections Contact
Dr. Peter Whiteley
Curator of North American Ethnology
Division of Anthropology
General phone: (212) 496-3496
Email: whiteley@amnh.org

Repatriation Contact
Nell Murphy
Director of Cultural Resources,
Division of Anthropology
Phone: (212) 769-5837
Email: nmurphy@amnh.org

Online collections search
amnh.org/our-research/anthropology

Research Access Policy-Collections & Archives
amnh.org/our-research/anthropology/policies-links/research-policy

AMNH repatriation stories
amnh.org/content/search?SearchText=repatriation

Washington, DC

Smithsonian National Museum of the American Indian

The Smithsonian Institute consists of numerous museums and other institutions that house several different collections. Of these institutions, the Smithsonian's National Museum of Natural History and the National Museum of the American Indian (NMAI) hold major collections of Indigenous Ancestors and belongings.

The NMAI actually has three locations. The main institution is located in Washington, DC. A secondary museum is located in New York City, and the NMAI's main storage facility is located within the museum's Cultural Resource Centre in Suitland, Maryland.

The NMAI does not follow NAGPRA, as the Smithsonian Institute has its own repatriation act for its museums holding major Indigenous collections: americanindian.si.edu/sites/1/files/pdf/about/NMAIAct.pdf

The museum also has a repatriation policy (see link below). For an overview of collections held in the Smithsonian National Museum of the American Indian, visit: americanindian.si.edu/explore/collections

Washington Address
National Museum of
the American Indian
National Mall
Fourth Street &
Independence Avenue SW
Washington, DC 20560
USA
Phone: (202) 633-1000
americanindian.si.edu/
visit/washington

New York Address
National Museum of
the American Indian
George Gustav Heye Center
1 Bowling Green
New York, NY, 10004
USA
Phone: (212) 514-3700
americanindian.si.edu/
visit/newyork

Maryland Address
National Museum of
the American Indian
Smithsonian Institution
Cultural Resources Center
4220 Silver Hill Road
Suitland-Silver Hill, MD
20746-2863
USA
Phone: (301) 238-1435
americanindian.si.edu/explore/collections/crc

Repatriation Contact
Repatriation Office, Cultural Resources Center
Phone: (301) 238-1548
Email: nmai-repatriation@si.edu

Collections Research Request
surveygizmo.com/s3/3009067/NMAI-Object-Collections-Research-Request (bit.ly/NMAIcollections)

Collections Database
collections.si.edu/search

Repatriation Overview
americanindian.si.edu/explore/collections/repatriation

Repatriation Policy
americanindian.si.edu/sites/1/files/pdf/repatriation/NMAI-RepatriationPolicy-2014-updated-2017.pdf

Step-by-Step Guide through the Repatriation Process
americanindian.si.edu/sites/1/files/pdf/repatriation/NMAI-RepatrationGuidelines-2014-updated-2017.pdf (bit.ly/NMAIstep)

Recovering Voices Community Research Grant
recoveringvoices.si.edu/resourcesandgrants/grants.html

Curatorial Residency Program
nmai.si.edu/connect/residencies

Internships for Post-secondary Students
nmai.si.edu/connect/internships

Smithsonian National Museum of Natural History

The Smithsonian National Museum of Natural History is also not bound to the Native American Graves Protection and Repatriation Act and follows the Smithsonian National Museum of the American Indian Act: americanindian.si.edu/sites/1/files/pdf/about/NMAIAct.pdf (bit.ly/PL101-185)

It also has its own repatriation policy (see below). For a general overview of collections held in this museum, visit: naturalhistory.si.edu/research/anthropology

Address
Smithsonian National Museum of Natural History
10th Street & Constitution Avenue NW
Washington, DC 20560
USA
Phone: (202) 633-1000
General inquiries: info@si.edu
naturalhistory.si.edu

Repatriation Office
naturalhistory2.si.edu/anthropology/repatriation/index.htm

Collections Search
naturalhistory.si.edu/research/anthropology/collections-and-archives-access

Arranging to Visit Collections
naturalhistory.si.edu/research/anthropology/collections-and-archives-access/anthropology-collections-appointment-request (bit.ly/AnthroCollections)

Repatriation Policy and Guidelines
naturalhistory2.si.edu/anthropology/repatriation/pdf/NMNH%20Repatriation%20Guidelines%20and%20Procedures%202012.pdf (bit.ly/NMAIguidelines)

Recovering Voices Community Research Grant
naturalhistory.si.edu/research/anthropology/programs/recovering-voices (bit.ly/RecoveringVoices)

Washington State

Seattle Art Museum

For an overview of collections held at the Seattle Art museum, visit:
art.seattleartmuseum.org/collections;jsessionid=975AD3F6AF3F6B88F50955DC3F649C9F (bit.ly/SAMhighlights)

Address
Seattle Art Museum
1300 First Avenue
Seattle, WA 98101-2003
USA
Phone: (206) 654-3100
seattleartmuseum.org

Curatorial Contact
Inquiries must be submitted by email or mail:
Curatorial Administrative Assistant
Seattle Art Museum
1300 First Avenue
Seattle, WA 98101-2003
USA
Email: submitting@seattleartmuseum.org

Collections Search
art.seattleartmuseum.org/collections/92391/native-american-art/objects

Library and Resources
seattleartmuseum.org/programs-and-learning/libraries-and-resources

Deaccessioning
Scroll down to the very end of the page for a brief overview
seattleartmuseum.org/collections/collection-resources

Internships
seattleartmuseum.org/about-sam/careers#int

University of Washington Burke Museum

For an overview of collections held at the Burke Museum, visit:
burkemuseum.org/research-and-collections/collections-databases

As well, check out the Burke Museum Bill Holm Center for the Study of Northwest Native Art:
burkemuseum.org/research-and-collections/bill-holm-center

Address
The Burke Museum
4300 15th Avenue NE
Seattle, WA 98105
USA
Phone: (206) 543-7907
Email: theburke@uw.edu
burkemuseum.org

Curatorial Contact
Sven Haakanson
Curator of Native American Anthropology
Phone: (206) 543-3210
Email: svenh@uw.edu

Collections

Kathy Dougherty
Collections Manager
Phone: (206) 543-6623
Email: kad33@uw.edu

Rebecca Andrews
Collections Manager
Phone: (206) 543-6623
Email: randrew@uw.edu

Repatriation Contact

Registrar
Phone: (206) 616-7318
Email: burkereg@uw.edu

Bill Holm Center

Kathryn Bunn-Marcuse
Curator of Northwest Native Art,
Director of Bill Holm Center
Phone: (206) 543-5344
Email: kbunn@uw.edu

Archaeology Contact

Archaeology Outreach
Phone: (206) 685-3849 ext. 1
Email: archy@uw.edu

Collections Search
burkemuseum.org/research-and-collections/collections-databases

Repatriation Overview
burkemuseum.org/research-and-collections/culture/services-and-policies/repatriation (bit.ly/BurkeRepatriate)

Bill Holm Centre Grants
burkemuseum.org/research-and-collections/bill-holm-center/grants

United Kingdom

Cambridge, England

Cambridge Museum of Anthropology and Archaeology

For an overview of collections held at the Cambridge Museum of Anthropology and Archaeology, visit: maa.cam.ac.uk/category/collections-2

Address
Museum of Archaeology and Anthropology
Downing Street
Cambridge, England CB2 3DZ
United Kingdom
Phone: +44 1223 333516
General inquiries: +44 1223 333510
Contact info:
maa.cam.ac.uk/category/about-the-museum-of-archaeology-and-anthropology-history-governance-job-opportunities-staff/contact-us (bit.ly/MAAcontact)

maa.cam.ac.uk

Initial Contact
Dr. Anita Herle
Senior Curator of World Anthropology (The Pacific and the Americas)
Email: ach13@cam.ac.uk

Anthropology Collections Contact
Rachel Hand
Collections Manager/Curatorial Assistant (Anthropology)
Email: rh259@cam.ac.uk

Archaeology Collections Contact
Imogen Gunn
Collections Manager/Curatorial
Assistant (Archaeology)
Email: ilg22@cam.ac.uk

Online Collections Search
collections.maa.cam.ac.uk/index.php?cmd=objects

Repatriation Info
maa.cam.ac.uk/category/about-the-museum-of
-archaeology-and-anthropology-history-governance-job
-opportunities-staff/repatriation (bit.ly/MAArepatriate)

Procedure for Handling Claims for the Transfer
of Stewardship of Human Remains
www.registrarysoffice.admin.cam.ac.uk/files/human
-remains-procedure.pdf (bit.ly/RemainsTransfer)

Guidelines for Consideration of Requests for Return of
Cultural Property
maa.cam.ac.uk/guidelines-for-consideration-of-requests
-for-return-of-cultural-property (bit.ly/ReturnGuidelines)

Exeter, England

Royal Albert Memorial Museum

For an overview of collections held at the Royal
Albert Memorial Museum, visit:
rammcollections.org.uk

Address
Royal Albert Memorial
Museum & Art Gallery
Queen Street
Exeter, England EX4 3RX
United Kingdom
Phone: +44 1392 265858
rammuseum.org.uk

Collections Contact
Tony Eccles
Curator of Ethnography
Phone: +44 1392 265312
Email: Tony.Eccles@
exeter.gov.uk

Collections Database
rammcollections.org.uk

Online Collections Search
swcollectionsexplorer.org.uk

Collections Development Policy
committees.exeter.gov.uk/documents/s33062/RAMM_collections_development_policy_final%2016012014%20Scrutiny%20Committee%20-%20Economy.pdf (bit.ly/CollectionsPolicy)

Liverpool, England

World Museum—National Museums of Liverpool

For an overview of collections held in National Museums of Liverpool, visit:
liverpoolmuseums.org.uk/wml/collections/ethnology/index.aspx

Address
World Museum—National Museums of Liverpool
William Brown Street
Liverpool, England L3 8EN
United Kingdom
Phone (information desk): +44 151 478 4393
General inquiries (email):

www.liverpoolmuseums.org.uk/about/contact/ContactForm .aspx?EnquiryID=24 (bit.ly/LiverpoolContact)

www.liverpoolmuseums.org.uk/wml/index.aspx

Ethnology Collections Contacts
Emma Martin
Senior Curator of Ethnology
Phone: +44 151 478 4330
Email: Emma.Martin@liverpoolmuseums.org.uk

Ethnology general email:
themuseum@liverpoolmuseums.org.uk

Request for the Return of Human Remains from National Museums Liverpool's Collections
Link for downloading document
liverpoolmuseums.org.uk/about/corporate/policies/human -remains-requests-for-return.doc (bit.ly/LiverpoolRequest)

Inventory of Human Remains
liverpoolmuseums.org.uk/about/corporate/policies/ human_remains_inventory.pdf (bit.ly/LiverpoolRemains)

Human Remains Policy
liverpoolmuseums.org.uk/about/corporate/policies/ human-remains-policy.doc (bit.ly/LiverpoolPolicy)

Collections Development Policy
liverpoolmuseums.org.uk/about/corporate/policies/collections -development-policy-NML-april2014.pdf (bit.ly/LiverpoolCDP)

Collections History
liverpoolmuseums.org.uk/wml/collections/ethnology/ americas-collections.pdf (bit.ly/LiverpoolCollectionHistory)

London, England

British Museum

For an overview of collections held in the British Museum, visit: britishmuseum.org/about_us/departments.aspx

Address
The British Museum
Great Russell Street
London, England WC1B 3DG
United Kingdom
General inquiries: info@britishmuseum.org
britishmuseum.org

Initial Staff Contact
Amber Lincoln, Curator of Americas
Phone: +44 20 7323 8028
Email: ALincoln@britishmuseum.org

Online Collections Database
britishmuseum.org/research/collection_online/search.aspx

British Museum Act
britishmuseum.org/PDF/BM1963Act.pdf

Amendment to the British Museum Act
publications.parliament.uk/pa/cm200910/cmbills/037/10037.i-i.html#j01 (bit.ly/BMA1963)

Human Remains Information
www.britishmuseum.org/about_us/management/human_remains.aspx?_ga=2.257389067.1030089722.1536255337-1892002795.1536255337 (bit.ly/BMhuman)

Policy on Human Remains
britishmuseum.org/PDF/HumanRemains.pdf

Deaccession of Objects from the Collection Policy
britishmuseum.org/pdf/De-accession%20Policy%20
July%202013%20FINAL.pdf (bit.ly/DeaccessionPolicy)

The Natural History Museum

For an overview of collection held in the Natural History Museum, visit:
nhm.ac.uk/discover/collections.html

Address
The Natural History Museum
Cromwell Road
London, England SW7 5BD
United Kingdom
General Inquiries: nhm.ac.uk/about-us/contact-enquiries/forms/emailform.jsp

nhm.ac.uk (bit.ly/NHMcontact)

Repatriation Contact
Dr. Heather Bonney
Principal Curator, Human Remains and Anthropology
nhm.ac.uk/contact-us/forms/emailform.jsp?recip=H.Bonney&business_title=Dr+Heather+Bonney
(bit.ly/HBonney)

Online Collections Database
data.nhm.ac.uk/?_ga=2.8710711.320434538.1547353543-8557638.1547264208 (bit.ly/NHMportal)

Oxford, England

Pitt Rivers Museum

For an overview of collections held in the Pitt Rivers Museum, visit:
prm.ox.ac.uk/collections

Address
Pitt Rivers Museum
South Parks Road
Oxford, England OX1 3PP
United Kingdom
General inquiries:
prm@prm.ox.ac.uk
prm.ox.ac.uk

Initial Staff Contact
Marina De Alarcón
Curator, Joint Head
of Collections
Email: marina.dealarcon@
prm.ox.ac.uk

Collections Contact
Collections general email: objects.colls@prm.ox.ac.uk

Online Collections Database
prm.ox.ac.uk/databases

About Pitt Rivers Human Remains Repatriation
prm.ox.ac.uk/human.html

Scotland

National Museum of Scotland

For an overview of the National Museum of Scotland's collections, visit:
nms.ac.uk/collections-research/our-collections

Address
National Museum of Scotland
Chambers Street
Edinburgh, Scotland EH1 1JF
United Kingdom
Phone: +44 300 123 6789
General list of contacts: nms.ac.uk/about-us/contact-us/#collections
nms.ac.uk/national-museum-of-scotland

Collections Contacts
Dr. Antje Denner
Principal Curator (Oceania,
Americas and Africa)
Email: a.denner@nms.ac.uk
General collections email:
collections@nms.ac.uk

Online Collections Search
nms.ac.uk/explore-our-collections/search-our-collections

Human Remains in Collections Policy
nms.ac.uk/media/1158202/human-remains
-in-collections-policy-2018.pdf

Guidelines for the Care of Human Remains
in Scottish Museum Collections
museumsgalleriesscotland.org.uk/media/1089/
guidelines-for-the-care-of-human-remains-in-scottish
-museum-collections.pdf (bit.ly/ScottishRemains)

Collections Development Strategy 2017–2022
nms.ac.uk/media/1154769/collections-development
-strategy-2017-2022-pdf-version.pdf (bit.ly/NMSdevelop)

Denmark

National Museum of Denmark (Nationalmuseet)

The National Museum of Denmark has museums across the country. For an overview of collections, visit:
en.natmus.dk/organisation/management-secretariat-and
-research-administration/modern-history-and-world-cultures/
ethnographic-collection (bit.ly/NMDethnographic)

Address
Nationalmuseet
Prinsens Palæ
Ny Vestergade 10
1471 København K (Copenhagen)
Denmark
Phone: +45 3313 4411
en.natmus.dk

Initial Contact
Mille Gabriel
Curator of North and South American Collections
Phone: +45 4120 6210
Email: mille.gabriel@natmus.dk

Ethnographic Collections Contacts
Knud Overgaard Pedersen
Ethnographic Collection Secretary
Phone: +45 4120 6201
Email: knudop@natmus.dk

Christian Sune Pedersen
Research and Development Manager
Phone: +45 4120 6200
Email: christian.sune.pedersen@natmus.dk

Collections Search
samlinger.natmus.dk/search?collection=ES&sort=modification%7Cdesc

Repatriation Information
Background: Beyond Repatriation
natmus.dk/organisation/forskning-samling-og-bevaring/nyere-tid-og-verdens-kulturer/etnografisk-samling/arktisk-forskning/about-sila/background (bit.ly/BeyondRepatriation)

Germany

Berlin

Staatliche Museen zu Berlin

The Staatliche Museen zu Berlin is an organization consisting of numerous museums and other institutions that house several different collections. Of these institutions, the Ethnologisches Museum holds collections originating from BC. For an overview of collections held at the Ethnologisches Museum, visit: www.smb.museum/en/museums-institutions/ethnologisches-museum/collection-research/about-the-collection.html (bit.ly/BerlinMuseum)

Address
Staatliche Museen zu Berlin
Education, Outreach, Visitor Services
Genthiner Straße 38
10785 Berlin, Germany
Phone: +49 30 266424242
Email: service@smb.museum
www.smb.museum/en/museums-institutions/ethnologisches-museum/about-us/profile.html (bit.ly/BerlinMuseumProfile)

Collections Contact
Monika Zessnik
Curator of North American Collections
Ethnologisches Museum
Email: m.zessnik@smb.spk-berlin.de

Online Collections Search
smb-digital.de/eMuseumPlus?service=ExternalInterface&module=collection&moduleFunction=highlight&filterName=filter.collection.highlights.1300 (bit.ly/SMBdigital)

Statement Regarding the Approach of the Stiftung Preußischer Kulturbesitz (Prussian Cultural Heritage Foundation) to Handling Human Remains in the Staatliche Museen zu Berlin (National Museums in Berlin) Collections
preussischer-kulturbesitz.de/fileadmin/user_upload/documents/mediathek/schwerpunkte/provenienz_eigentum/rp/151001_Grundposition_Human_Remains_eng.pdf (bit.ly/NMBhuman)

Media: Restitution to Alaska Natives
preussischer-kulturbesitz.de/en/newsroom/dossiers-and-news/all-dossiers/dossier-provenienzforschung/grave-goods-from-alaska.html (bit.ly/AlaskaGraves)

Media: Ethnologisches Museum Returns Objects to Alaska Natives
preussischer-kulturbesitz.de/fileadmin/user_upload/documents/presse/pressemitteilungen/2018/180516_Restitution-Chugach-Ceremony_EN.pdf (bit.ly/AlaskaReturn)

Fellowship Programs
www.smb.museum/en/research/scholarship-programmes.html

Dresden

Museum of Ethnology (Museum für Völkerkunde)

The Museum für Völkerkunde is one of three ethnological museums within the greater Staatliche Kunstsammlungen Dresden (SKD) institution. The contacts provided below also manage collections in the GRASSI Museum für Völkerkunde zu Leipzig (GRASSI Museum of Ethnology in Leipzig) and the Völkerkundemuseum Herrnhut (Ethnographic Museum in Herrnhut), which hold materials from the Northwest Coast. For an overview of collections held in the Museum für Völkerkunde, visit: voelkerkunde-dresden.skd.museum/en

Address
Museum für Völkerkunde
Japanisches Palais
Palaisplatz 11
01097 Dresden
Germany
Phone: +49 351 49 14 2000
Email: besucherservice@skd.museum
voelkerkunde-dresden.skd.museum/en

Collections Contact
Dr. Frank Usbeck
Researcher (American Collections)
Phone: +49 341 9731-902
Email: frank.usbeck@skd.museum

Collections Search
skd-online-collection.skd.museum

Media: Dresden Museum of Ethnology Returns Ancestral Remains to Native Hawaiian Group
metropolism.com/nl/news/33393_dresden_museum_of_ethnology_returns_ancestral_remains_to_native_hawaiian_group

Research and Study Programs
www.skd.museum/en/research/#c4803

Netherlands

Leiden

National Museum of Ethnology (Museum Volkenkunde)

For a general overview of collections held at the National Museum of Ethnology, visit: volkenkunde.nl/en/about-volkenkunde/collection

Address
Museum Volkenkunde
Steenstraat 1
2312 BS Leiden
Netherlands
General inquiries (email):
info@volkenkunde.nl
volkenkunde.nl/en/

Collections general email:
collectie@wereldculturen.nl

Henrietta Lidchi
Chief Curator
Phone: +31 88 00 42 922
Email: henrietta.lidchi@wereldculturen.nl

Collections Contact
Cindy Zalm
Head of Collections Management
Phone: +31 88 00 42 985
Email: cindy.zalm@wereldculturen.nl

Online Collections Search
collectie.wereldculturen.nl/?query=search=packages=OnViewRV#/query/f2f995ab-e091-440a-8d31-2ec25e0559f5 (bit.ly/NMVWsearch)

Research Centre for Material Culture
materialculture.nl/en/research

APPENDIX H

Resources on Education in Indigenous Museology

Museum Training Programs and Internships

Bill Holm Center
Northwest Native Art research, workshops, mentor-apprenticeship grant
burkemuseum.org/research-and-collections/bill-holm-center

Canadian Conservation Institute
Training and workshops
canada.ca/en/conservation-institute.html

Canadian Museum of History
RBC Indigenous Internship Program
historymuseum.ca/learn/research/the-rbc-aboriginal-training-program-in-museum-practices/#tabs (bit.ly/RBCtraining)

Smithsonian National Museum of the American Indian
Internships, residencies, training, workshops, etc.
americanindian.si.edu/connect

Union of BC Indian Chiefs
Claims research course
learning.ubcic.bc.ca

YVR Art Foundation
Artist grants, masterpiece study travel grant
yvraf.com

Post-Secondary Education

Algonquin College of Applied Arts and Technology
Museum Technology Program
algonquincollege.com

Haida Gwaii Higher Education Society
Semester in Reconciliation
hghes.ca/reconciliation-studies

National Trust for Canada
List of conservation programs across Canada
archive.nationaltrustcanada.ca/resources/
education/conservation-programs

Queen's University
Art History and Art Conservation
queensu.ca/art/art-conservation

University of British Columbia
Masters of Archival Studies, First Nations
Curriculum Concentration
slais.ubc.ca/programs/degrees/mas

University of Victoria
Indigenous Co-operative Education
uvic.ca/services/indigenous/students/supports/co-op/index.php

Cultural Resource Management Program
continuingstudies.uvic.ca/culture-museums-and-indigenous-studies/programs/cultural-resource-management (bit.ly/UVicCRM)

Fellowships

Peabody Essex Museum
Native American Fellowship Program
pem.org/employment/native-american-fellowship-program/about-our--program (bit.ly/PEMabout)

Smithsonian Institute
smithsonianofi.com/fellowship-opportunities

Education Kits

UBC Museum of Anthropology
Repatriation Teaching Kit
moa.ubc.ca/wp-content/uploads/TeachingKit-Repatriation.pdf

Museum, Archival and Archaeological Associations

Associations are professional membership organizations that exist around the world both nationally and regionally to advance the heritage sector. For example, the Canadian Museums Association "works for the recognition, growth, and stability of the sector" and represents "Canadian museum professionals both within Canada and internationally."[10] These associations offer opportunities to attend or present at conferences (a great place to network and educate about repatriation), grant programs, professional development programs,

10 Canadian Museums Association, "About the CMA," museums.ca/site/about

etc. You generally have to be associated with a museum or heritage institution to join, but either way, they are great organizations to connect with for repatriation advocacy or other support.

Archives Association of British Columbia
aabc.ca

Association of Canadian Archivists
archivists.ca

British Columbia Association of Professional Archaeologists
bcapa.ca

British Columbia Museums Association
museumsassn.bc.ca

Canadian Archaeological Association
canadianarchaeology.com

Canadian Museums Association
museums.ca

Western Museums Association
westmuse.org

APPENDIX I

Frequently Asked Questions about Repatriation

General Questions about Repatriation

Q What does repatriation mean?

A Repatriation is the return to the country of origin. For museums, repatriation applies more specifically to the return of human remains and cultural objects to Indigenous communities.

Q What is digital repatriation?

A Digital repatriation is the return of items of cultural heritage in a digital format to the communities from which they originated. The term is often applied to museum, library and archives collections, and can refer to digitized photographs, documents, film and audio recordings.

Questions Specific to the Royal BC Museum

Q Do I need to pay to visit the Royal BC Museum?

A No, Indigenous people can self-identify as Indigenous at the ticket office for free access to the galleries. For a behind-the-scenes tour of the Indigenous collection, there is no cost either, but you are required to make an appointment. It is also advisable to make an appointment if you require assistance looking at Indigenous materials in the Archives. To set up an appointment with Collections and Archives, contact:

Brian Seymour, Collections Manager, Anthropology
Email: bseymour@royalbcmuseum.bc.ca
Phone: (250) 387-2440

Dr. Genevieve Hill, Collections Manager
and Researcher, Anthropology
Email: ghill@royalbcmuseum.bc.ca
Phone: (250) 893-8019

Genevieve Weber, Archivist
Email: gweber@royalbcmuseum.bc.ca
Phone: (250) 886-4017

Q How can I contact the Indigenous Collections and Repatriation Department?

A You can contact the Indigenous Collections and Repatriation Department at:

Lou-ann Neel, Repatriation Specialist, Royal BC Museum
Email: lneel@royalbcmuseum.bc.ca
Phone: (250) 889-9674

Royal BC Museum Repatriation Requests

Q How does my Nation begin a repatriation request at the Royal BC Museum?

A Contact the repatriation specialist to discuss your repatriation request. The process usually begins with a visit to the Royal BC Museum and with a determination that this request falls under the Royal BC Museum Indigenous Collections and Repatriation Policy or under Treaty.

Q Does the Royal BC Museum provide funding for consultations and repatriations?

A Yes. With the support of the provincial government, the Royal BC Museum manages a repatriation grant program. Contact the repatriation specialist for further details. For those in the Treaty process, the consultation may be covered under the Treaty agreement.

Q What can be repatriated?

A There are three main categories of collections that can be repatriated. Ancestral remains and burial objects are a repatriation priority for the Royal BC Museum. According to the Royal BC Museum Indigenous Collections and Repatriation Policy, any Indigenous cultural objects that were acquired during the Potlatch Ban from 1885 to 1951 are considered to have come into the collection under duress and can be repatriated. The Royal BC Museum is also actively digitizing the archival photographs and audio recordings to return to Indigenous communities.

Q Who is eligible to make a repatriation claim to the Royal BC Museum?

A Tribal councils, band councils or repatriation committees that have been designated by their tribal authorities. The Royal BC Museum does not repatriate to individuals.

Royal BC Museum Questions about Collections

Q How many Indigenous items are in the Royal BC Museum?

A There are over 200,000 archaeological objects, 14,000 cultural objects and 20,000 audiovisual objects.

Q What is the total number of human remains in the Royal BC Museum, and how were they acquired?

A There are approximately 700 Ancestral remains in the museum. Almost all of them are Indigenous. They have come into the collection through archaeological digs, collectors, the RCMP and the coroner's office. We do not actively collect Ancestral remains, and we strongly support the repatriation of Ancestral remains.

Q How many Ancestral remains have already been repatriated?

A The Royal BC Museum has repatriated over 1,000 Ancestral remains in the last three decades.

Q How many Indigenous objects have already been repatriated?

A Hundreds of cultural objects have been repatriated, most of them through the Treaty process. Some highlights include a totem pole to the Haida, hundreds of cultural objects to the Nisga'a, and a screen and 50 other belongings to the Huu-ay-aht.

Q Is there a cost to get copies of photographs and audio recordings?

A In response to the Calls to Action of the Truth and Reconciliation Commission, the Royal BC Museum has decided to waive fees for personal use of photographs and audio recordings by Indigenous people. There is a queue, so your requests may take time to process.

Q Are Indigenous communities required to build museums or repositories in order to repatriate cultural objects from museums?

A It is not mandatory, although Indigenous communities do have a strong desire to house cultural belongings in safe environments including cultural centres, schools and tribal offices. The Royal BC Museum does not stipulate that cultural belongings be repatriated to a museum or repository, but we are willing to advise on museological standards.

APPENDIX J

Repatriation Success Stories

Some Nations have been working in repatriation for decades; others are just starting out. For some inspiration and to learn about the Indigenous repatriation movement, check out some of these success stories.

Publications

***BC Studies* no. 199, Autumn 2018: Indigeneities and Museums: Ongoing Conversations**
Guest editors Caitlin Gordon-Walker and Dr. Martha Black
bcstudies.com/?q=issues/item/bc-studies-no-199-autumn-2018

Raven Travelling: Two Centuries of Haida Art
Daina Augaitis (editor), Douglas & McIntyre, 2008
See Lucy Bell and Vince Collison, "Repatriation of Haida Ancestors and the Rebirth of Ourselves"

Returning the Past: Repatriation of First Nations Cultural Property
moa.ubc.ca/wp-content/uploads/TeachingKit-Repatriation.pdf

The Force of Family: Repatriation, Kinship, and Memory on Haida Gwaii
Cara Krmpotich, University of Toronto Press, 2014

We Are Coming Home: Repatriation and the Restoration of Blackfoot Cultural Confidence
Gerald T. Conaty, Athabasca University Press, 2015

aupress.ca/books/120242/ebook/99Z_Conaty_2015-We_Are_Coming_Home.pdf (bit.ly/WeAreComingHome)

The Routledge Companion to Indigenous Repatriation: Return, Reconcile, Renew
Cressida Fforde, Honor Keeler and Tim McKeown (editors), Routledge, (forthcoming)
See Nika Collison and Cara Krmpotich, "Saahlinda Naay—Saving Things House: The Haida Gwaii Museum Past, Present and Future"

Documentaries

***1491: The Untold Story of the Americas Before Columbus*, Episode 8: "Continuance"**
aptn.ca/1491

Box of Treasures
umista.ca

Heiltsuk Ancestors Return Home to Rest in Namu, 2011
youtube.com/watch?v=8qCOpcGRp4g

"Museums: Repatriation and Ownership"
The Agenda with Steve Paikin, TVO News
tvo.org/video/programs/the-agenda-with-steve-paikin/museums-repatriation-and-ownership (bit.ly/TVOmuseums)

National Film Board Repatriation Shorts
nfb.ca/indigenous-cinema/subjects/community/repatriation-return-of-objects-materials-to-communities/?&film_lang=en (bit.ly/NFBrepatriation)

Stolen Spirits of Haida Gwaii
Primitive Entertainment, 2005
www.isuma.tv/node/70195
www.primitive.net

The New Collectors
Ravens & Eagles Productions, 2003
Part 1 (clip): youtube.com/watch?v=HjiM9kFgES0
Part 2 (clip): youtube.com/watch?v=8r6ym40E2hE
Distributor:
movingimages.ca/store/products.php?ravens_eagles_new_collectors_one

The Return of the G'psgolox Pole
youtube.com/watch?reload=9&v=05C5Ub19exM

Indigenous Nations with Repatriation Experience

Many Indigenous Nations are involved in repatriation of Ancestral remains, cultural belongings and intangible heritage. One of the best-known examples of repatriation of cultural belongings is with the Kwakwaka'wakw Nation. For more information on the Potlatch Collection, visit the U'mista Cultural Centre's website (umista.ca) and the Nuyumbalees Cultural Centre's website (nuyumbalees.com). To learn about the Haida repatriation journey, another well-known journey, see the case study in Part 7: Case Study: Repatriation Journey of the Haida Nation and check out the documentaries *The New Collectors* and *Stolen Spirits of Haida Gwaii*, above.

Some BC Indigenous Nations have repatriated through the Treaty process, including the Nisga'a Nation (nisgaamuseum.ca), Tla'amin (tlaaminnation.com) and the Manuulth (maanulth.ca)

As well, 21 Nations received repatriation grants through the Royal BC Museum in 2018. Watch for the Royal BC Museum Indigenous biannual newsletter and the website (rbcm.ca) for updates from active repatriation Indigenous groups.

Additional Resources

Several published resources are available online and in print that cover a variety of topics on repatriation. Here are a few to get you started:

Publications

A Guide to International Repatriation: Starting an Initiative in Your Community
Honor Keeler, Association on American Indian Affairs
indian-affairs.org/uploads/8/7/3/8/87380358/international_repatriation_guide.pdf (bit.ly/InternationalRepatriate)

Finding Our Way Home: A Handbook for Tribes, Universities, Museums and Individuals Working toward Repatriation under NAGPRA
Little Traverse Bay Bands of Odawa Indians
Repatriation, Archives and Records Department
www.ltbbodawa-nsn.gov/Arch/NAGPRA%20LTBB%20Manual.pdf

This Is Our Life: Haida Material Heritage and Changing Museum Practice
Cara Krmpotich, Laura Peers and the Haida Repatriation Committee, UBC Press, 2014

Websites

Several resources are available on the internet related to the shared history of Indigenous Peoples and Canada. Here are a couple to get you started:

***Haida Laas:* "Smallpox Journal"**
Focused on Haida Ancestors who died from smallpox
haidanation.ca/wp-content/uploads/2017/03/jl_mar.09.pdf

Stone T'xwelátse
srrmcentre.com/StoneTxwelatse/15Sqwelqwel.html

***SFU IPinCH:* "Repatriating Indigenous Cultural Heritage—What's Reconciliation Got to Do With It?"**
sfu.ca/ipinch/outputs/blog/repatriating-indigenous-cultural-heritage-what-s-reconciliation-got-do-it (bit.ly/IPinCHrepatriate)

Searching for Our Heritage
Yukon Department of Tourism and Culture Museum Resources
tc.gov.yk.ca/museum_resources.html

Haida Repatriation Committee
repatriation.ca